AI Longevity Economics

How Longer Lifespans Will Reshape Healthcare, Work, Retirement, and Wealth

By Joe Correa

Published by Live Stronger Faster

This book is for educational and informational purposes only. The author and publisher are not engaged in rendering legal, financial, or other professional advice. Readers should consult a qualified professional before making any medical or financial decisions.

First Edition

Table of Contents

Introduction

For most of human history, economics quietly assumed one unchanging truth: human life is short, productivity peaks early, decline is inevitable, and retirement marks the end of economic relevance. Entire financial systems—healthcare, insurance, pensions, labor markets, taxation, education, housing, and wealth planning—were built on the expectation that the average person would live a relatively brief life, work for a few decades, and then slowly exit the productive economy. Artificial intelligence is now dismantling that assumption at its foundation. As AI-driven longevity technologies extend healthspan, delay disease, and potentially push average lifespans far beyond what any modern system was designed to support, humanity is entering an unprecedented economic transition—one where time itself becomes the most valuable, destabilizing, and unequal asset of all. This book explores that transition not as speculation, but as an unavoidable economic reckoning already unfolding beneath the surface of global markets.

Longevity has always had economic implications, but AI transforms longevity from a biological outcome into an engineered variable. Predictive health models, AI-guided diagnostics, personalized prevention systems, and machine-learning-driven drug discovery are rapidly shifting medicine from reactive care to proactive optimization. As illness is delayed and vitality extended, the economic cost curves of healthcare begin to bend—but not evenly. Systems designed to manage disease late in life now face the paradox of sustaining people who remain healthy, cognitively capable, and productive for far longer than anticipated. This creates both extraordinary opportunity and profound disruption. Longer lives mean longer careers, extended earning potential, prolonged consumption, and greater cumulative wealth creation. At the same time, they strain social safety nets, redefine retirement, challenge intergenerational wealth transfer, and force governments to confront fiscal models that no longer align with biological reality.

The economics of longevity is not simply about living longer—it is about who gets to live longer, under what conditions, and at what cost. AI-driven longevity solutions are emerging first in high-income regions, private healthcare systems, and elite research institutions. Early access is expensive, data-driven, and unevenly distributed. As with every technological revolution before it, the benefits will initially accrue to those with capital, education, and infrastructure. This creates a new axis of inequality: lifespan inequality. In a world where some individuals routinely live to ninety, one hundred, or beyond with sustained cognitive and physical capacity, while others remain trapped in cycles of preventable disease and early mortality, longevity itself becomes a form of inherited and purchased advantage. The economic consequences of this divide will ripple through labor markets, insurance systems, real estate, political power, and social cohesion in ways few policymakers are prepared to manage.

Healthcare economics sits at the epicenter of this shift. Traditional healthcare models are built on episodic treatment, late-stage intervention, and reimbursement structures tied to procedures rather than prevention. AI-driven longevity upends this framework by prioritizing early detection, continuous monitoring, and long-term optimization. While this approach promises to reduce catastrophic healthcare spending associated with chronic disease, it also introduces new cost structures centered on subscriptions, data services, AI platforms, and personalized intervention pipelines. Healthcare spending does not disappear—it migrates. The winners in this new economy will not necessarily be hospitals or pharmaceutical giants alone, but technology platforms that own health data, predictive models, and longitudinal patient insights. The economic power of AI in longevity lies not just in curing disease, but in monetizing foresight.

Work and productivity will also be fundamentally reshaped by longer, healthier lives. The concept of a single career followed by retirement becomes economically obsolete in a world where people may remain capable of high-level work well into their seventies or eighties. Instead, the future favors multi-phase careers, recurring education, and lifelong skill renewal. AI accelerates this transition by lowering the barrier to retraining, automating cognitive labor, and augmenting human performance. The result is a labor market where age becomes less relevant than adaptability, and experience compounds rather than depreciates. However, this also intensifies competition across generations. Younger workers may find themselves competing with older, more experienced individuals who no longer exit the workforce on a predictable timeline. Without structural adaptation, this tension risks widening generational divides and destabilizing employment systems.

Retirement, as currently defined, may be the most fragile economic institution in the age of AI longevity. Pension systems, social security programs, and retirement savings models assume a limited post-work lifespan. Extending that lifespan by decades without redefining contribution structures or payout timelines renders these systems mathematically unsustainable. Governments face an uncomfortable choice: raise retirement ages, reduce benefits, increase taxes, or fundamentally redesign how value is created and distributed across a longer life. AI offers tools to manage this complexity—predictive fiscal modeling, dynamic policy simulation, and personalized retirement planning—but it cannot eliminate the political and social resistance inherent in changing deeply ingrained expectations about aging and entitlement.

Wealth accumulation takes on new dimensions when time horizons expand. Compounding over a longer lifespan dramatically increases the disparity between those who begin early and those who fall behind. AI-driven financial planning, algorithmic investing, and personalized wealth optimization will amplify this effect by improving efficiency and decision-making for those who can access these tools. At the same time, extended lifespans delay inheritance, reshape estate planning, and alter the flow of capital between generations. Families may span five or six living generations simultaneously, complicating traditional models of wealth transfer, caregiving, and economic dependency. The economic unit of the family itself evolves, becoming more complex, more interdependent, and more financially stratified.

On a macroeconomic scale, AI-driven longevity challenges assumptions about population growth, consumption patterns, and economic productivity. Longer lives do not automatically mean larger populations, but they do change age distributions, dependency ratios, and long-term demand structures. Housing markets must adapt to multi-decade occupancy, age-diverse communities, and evolving care needs. Urban planning must account for populations that remain active far longer than before. Education systems must shift from front-loaded models to continuous, modular learning architectures. AI becomes the connective tissue enabling this adaptation, coordinating data across sectors and optimizing systems that were never designed to operate on century-long timelines.

Yet alongside opportunity lies systemic risk. If longevity gains outpace institutional reform, economic instability becomes inevitable. Healthcare systems could collapse under mismatched incentives. Labor markets could stagnate under generational congestion. Wealth inequality could harden into biological inequality. Political systems could fracture as policy struggles to keep pace with technological reality. AI, while a catalyst for longevity, also accelerates these risks by increasing the speed at which change occurs. The same predictive models that optimize health can expose fiscal vulnerabilities. The same automation that enhances productivity can displace workers unprepared for longer careers. Managing longevity economics requires intentional design, ethical governance, and proactive investment in adaptability—not reactive crisis management.

This book is not a forecast—it is a framework. AI Longevity Economics examines how longer lifespans will reshape healthcare financing, redefine work and retirement, transform wealth creation, and alter the balance of economic power at both individual and societal levels. It equips readers to understand not only where these forces are heading, but how to position themselves, their families, businesses, and institutions within this emerging reality. Longevity is no longer a philosophical aspiration or a distant scientific goal—it is an economic variable entering balance sheets, policy models, and personal financial plans today.

The age of AI-powered longevity demands a new kind of economic literacy—one that recognizes time as capital, health as infrastructure, and adaptability as the ultimate currency. Those who understand this shift early will not merely live longer; they will live better positioned lives in a world where the meaning of work, wealth, and aging is being rewritten in real time. This book begins that understanding.

Chapter 1

Longevity as Economic Capital: How Time, Healthspan, and AI Are Redefining Wealth

For most of recorded history, wealth has been measured in tangible assets: land, currency, commodities, labor, and later knowledge. Time, although universally valuable, was never formally treated as an economic asset because it was scarce, unpredictable, and biologically constrained. Human lifespan placed a hard ceiling on how much value an individual could accumulate, produce, or influence. Artificial intelligence is now altering that constraint. As AI-driven longevity technologies extend healthy lifespan and compress disease, time itself begins to behave like capital—expandable, investable, and compounding. This transformation shifts the foundation of economics from resource scarcity toward lifespan scalability, where the duration of productive life becomes one of the most powerful determinants of wealth.

Economic systems implicitly assume biological decline. Education is concentrated in youth because learning capacity was thought to peak early. Career structures emphasize early productivity because experience eventually collides with aging limitations. Retirement systems assume a predictable decline in capability. Financial planning models compress wealth accumulation into a few decades of peak earning. AI longevity challenges each of these assumptions by extending cognitive performance, physical function, and adaptive capacity across far longer periods. When individuals remain capable of learning, creating, and producing value deep into later life, the temporal boundary of economic participation expands dramatically. Wealth creation no longer depends solely on income rate; it depends on duration of productive engagement. Time multiplies output.

The concept of longevity as economic capital rests on three reinforcing pillars: extended healthspan, sustained cognitive capacity, and continuous adaptability. AI contributes to each pillar simultaneously. Predictive health systems delay disease onset, preserving physiological function. Neuroadaptive technologies and AI-augmented cognition maintain learning speed and decision quality. Continuous education platforms powered by AI enable rapid skill acquisition at any age. Together these forces convert aging from a period of decline into a prolonged phase of capability. Economically, this means individuals retain earning potential, entrepreneurial capacity, and creative output across decades that were previously associated with retirement or dependency. The longer productive lifespan becomes, the greater the compounding effect on wealth.

Compounding is the central mechanism linking longevity and economics. Financial compounding has long been understood: investments grow exponentially over time. Longevity introduces biological compounding, where sustained health and cognitive performance enable extended economic activity, which in turn generates additional resources to further sustain health. AI accelerates this loop by improving decision-making in both health and finance. Individuals can optimize prevention, investment, and career strategy simultaneously across longer horizons. The result is not merely incremental wealth growth but multiplicative advantage. A person who remains economically active for sixty years rather than thirty does not simply double output; they gain decades of compounded learning, network expansion, and capital accumulation. Time amplifies capability.

However, longevity capital is not distributed equally. Access to AI-driven health optimization, preventive medicine, cognitive augmentation, and adaptive education varies by geography, income, and institutional infrastructure. Those with early access extend productive lifespan sooner, allowing compounding advantages to accumulate across generations. Those without access remain bound by traditional lifespan limits. This divergence introduces a structural economic gradient based on time itself. In such a world, inequality is no longer measured only in wealth or income but in years of healthy productivity. The economic distance between individuals may reflect decades of functional lifespan difference. Longevity becomes both asset and privilege.

Work structures must evolve to accommodate longevity capital. Traditional career arcs assume entry, peak, and exit within a fixed timeline. Extended productive lifespan dissolves this arc into multiple phases of learning, creation, and reinvention. Individuals may pursue several careers sequentially, interspersed with periods of education and recovery. AI facilitates these transitions by mapping skill transferability, predicting labor demand, and personalizing training pathways. Economically, this produces a more fluid workforce where experience accumulates rather than depreciates. Employers increasingly value adaptability and long-term capability rather than chronological age. The boundary between education and employment blurs into continuous development. Longevity capital expresses itself through sustained employability.

Entrepreneurship particularly benefits from extended lifespan. Venture creation often requires years of iteration, failure, and learning before success emerges. Longer healthy lives increase the probability that individuals can experiment across multiple ventures, refine strategy, and build networks over extended periods. AI tools reduce operational friction, enabling individuals of any age to launch and scale enterprises with minimal infrastructure. The combination of extended time and reduced barriers amplifies entrepreneurial output across the lifespan. Economically, this diversifies innovation sources and redistributes opportunity toward individuals who previously aged out of risk-taking phases. Longevity capital fuels persistent creativity.

Financial systems also adapt to longer horizons. Investment strategies optimized for thirty-year careers become suboptimal when individuals expect sixty or seventy productive years. Asset allocation shifts toward long-duration growth, multi-stage income streams, and adaptive withdrawal models. AI-driven financial planning integrates health predictions, career projections, and lifespan estimates into dynamic portfolios that evolve over decades. Insurance products begin to price not only mortality but healthspan trajectory. Retirement transforms into phased financial independence rather than permanent work cessation. Time becomes an explicit variable in financial design, treated as an adjustable resource rather than fixed endpoint.

Healthcare economics intersects directly with longevity capital because healthspan determines the usability of time. Years lived with disease or impairment contribute less economic value than years lived with vitality. AI extends the proportion of life spent in high-functioning states by enabling early detection, personalized intervention, and lifestyle optimization. As a result, not only lifespan but productive lifespan expands. The economic value of each additional year depends on its functional quality. Longevity capital therefore combines duration with performance. A decade of healthy productivity contributes exponentially more value than a decade of decline. AI shifts years from low-value to high-value states.

At the societal level, treating longevity as capital reframes policy priorities. Investments in preventive health, lifelong education, and adaptive labor markets become drivers of national productivity rather than social expenditure. Governments historically treated aging populations as fiscal burdens due to healthcare and pension costs. Extended healthspan reverses this perception by preserving productivity. AI-enabled longevity transforms aging populations into experienced, capable economic participants. Nations that successfully cultivate longevity capital may sustain growth despite demographic aging, while those that fail to adapt face stagnation. Longevity becomes a macroeconomic advantage.

Yet longevity capital introduces complex ethical and structural challenges. If time becomes a source of economic power, disparities in access translate into disparities in opportunity. Intergenerational dynamics shift as older individuals remain active longer, potentially delaying advancement for younger cohorts. Institutions designed around predictable generational turnover must adapt to extended participation across age groups. AI-mediated longevity also raises questions about valuation of human contribution: how should societies balance extended productivity with equitable opportunity? Economic systems must ensure that longevity capital enhances collective prosperity rather than concentrating advantage. Designing inclusive longevity economies becomes a central policy challenge.

The emergence of longevity as economic capital ultimately reframes wealth itself. Wealth is no longer only accumulated resources; it is the capacity to create value across time. Healthspan sustains capability, AI amplifies output, and extended lifespan multiplies both. Individuals who understand this shift can intentionally invest in longevity capital through health optimization, continuous learning, and adaptive career strategy. Societies that recognize it can redesign institutions to harness extended human potential. The future economy will not simply reward productivity—it will reward sustained productivity. Time, once a constraint, becomes the most powerful multiplier of human value. Longevity capital defines the economic frontier of the AI age.

The Long Horizon

Elena had always believed that life moved in chapters that closed behind you. Childhood, education, career, retirement—the sequence seemed natural and irreversible. Her father had retired at sixty-two and declined rapidly within a decade, his world shrinking from work colleagues and daily routines to medical appointments and quiet afternoons. Elena assumed her own path would follow the same arc. She built a stable career in finance, saved diligently, and envisioned retirement as a gentle descent into slower years. Time felt like something to endure and conserve, not expand.

In her mid-forties, Elena encountered the first fracture in that assumption. A routine health assessment offered by her employer included an AI-driven longevity analysis platform that integrated biomarkers, genetic predispositions, lifestyle metrics, and cognitive testing. The report did not simply estimate lifespan; it mapped projected healthspan across decades. According to the model, Elena had a high probability of remaining cognitively sharp and physically capable well into her eighties if she followed targeted interventions. The platform outlined personalized nutrition adjustments, sleep optimization, strength training protocols, and cognitive skill expansion pathways. For the first time, aging appeared not as a slope downward but as a horizon stretching forward.

At first she dismissed it as optimistic technology marketing. Yet over the next year she implemented small changes—resistance training twice weekly, structured sleep timing, micronutrient calibration, and digital cognitive exercises. Follow-up assessments showed measurable improvements: increased muscle density, faster reaction times, and enhanced memory recall. More surprising was her energy. Tasks that once exhausted her became manageable. Her concentration deepened. The sense of approaching decline that had quietly shadowed her forties receded. She began to feel time not as diminishing but as widening.

This shift in perception altered her professional life. Previously she had viewed her career trajectory as nearing its plateau. Advancement would slow; expertise would eventually become outdated. Now she reconsidered. If she might remain capable for another forty years, what was truly fixed? She enrolled in an AI-driven financial analytics certification designed for mid-career professionals. The adaptive learning platform adjusted pace and complexity to her performance, accelerating where she excelled and reinforcing where she lagged. Within months she acquired skills that once required years of formal training. Her confidence returned—not youthful confidence based on potential, but experienced confidence amplified by renewed capability. Elena's work began to change. She proposed integrating predictive modeling into her firm's long-term investment strategies, emphasizing extended lifespan trends and longevity economics. Colleagues initially saw the idea as niche, but demographic projections and emerging healthcare data supported her thesis. As populations aged more slowly and remained productive longer, consumption patterns, housing demand, and retirement assets would shift. Elena built models reflecting extended earning periods and delayed wealth transfer. Clients responded with enthusiasm. Her specialization in longevity-informed finance positioned her at the forefront of an emerging field.

Years passed, but Elena did not feel them accumulate in the way she once expected. Her body strengthened through consistent training. Cognitive agility remained high through continuous learning. Each year added not limitation but refinement. She launched a consultancy focused on longevity-based financial planning, advising individuals expecting multi-decade careers and extended retirement horizons. Her clients ranged from entrepreneurs in their fifties launching second ventures to professionals in their sixties planning new educational paths. Elena saw a pattern: when people recognized that their productive lifespan might double, their ambitions expanded accordingly.

Her relationship with time transformed completely. Instead of compressing goals into immediate decades, she layered them across long arcs. She pursued advanced certifications not for quick promotion but for mastery. She invested in ventures with extended maturation timelines. She mentored younger professionals without fearing obsolescence, knowing her own growth would continue alongside theirs. Time ceased to be a dwindling resource and became a field of opportunity stretching ahead. Longevity capital was no longer abstract; it was experiential.

In her seventies, Elena remained professionally active, though by then work had become elective rather than necessary. Her consultancy evolved into an advisory network shaping financial frameworks for extended lifespan societies. Governments and institutions sought guidance on adapting retirement systems and investment models. Elena, once anticipating quiet decline, now contributed to systemic transformation. Her insight did not stem solely from data but from lived extension—the understanding that capability can persist when cultivated intentionally.

Looking back, Elena realized the pivotal change had not been technological alone. AI tools enabled health optimization and accelerated learning, but the deeper shift was cognitive: recognizing time as expandable potential rather than finite countdown. That realization altered her decisions decades earlier, compounding across years into expertise, influence, and fulfillment. Her life illustrated the central truth of longevity economics: when healthy years expand, human ambition expands with them. Wealth becomes measured not only in assets but in sustained capacity to create value.

On a clear autumn morning at eighty-one, Elena walked along the waterfront near her home, her stride steady and posture upright. She reviewed a proposal from a global pension consortium exploring adaptive retirement ages based on healthspan metrics. The work remained complex, but she felt neither rushed nor diminished. Ahead lay projects, conversations, and discoveries still unfolding. The horizon remained open.

Elena paused and watched the sun rise over the water. She thought of her father, whose later years had narrowed prematurely, constrained by the expectations of his era. She wished he could have seen what she now understood: that time, when protected and extended, becomes the greatest form of wealth a human being can possess. Not merely years lived, but years lived capable. She turned back toward the city, moving with purpose into another day of a life still expanding.

Chapter 2

The Extended Workforce: How Longer Healthy Lives Are Transforming Careers, Productivity, and the Nature of Work

For more than a century, the structure of work has been organized around an implicit biological timeline: education in youth, peak productivity in midlife, and withdrawal from the workforce in older age. This sequence reflected not merely social convention but physiological reality. Physical endurance declined, cognitive speed slowed, and chronic disease increased with age, limiting long-term participation in demanding roles. Artificial intelligence–enabled longevity disrupts this foundational assumption by extending the period during which individuals remain cognitively capable, physically functional, and adaptively productive. As healthy lifespan lengthens, the workforce expands temporally, creating an extended workforce in which careers span far longer durations and participation persists across decades once associated with retirement.

The extended workforce is not simply a demographic shift; it is a structural transformation of economic participation. When individuals can remain capable into their seventies or eighties, labor supply increases not through population growth but through duration of engagement. Economically, this alters productivity curves, dependency ratios, and career trajectories. Traditional models assumed that experience would eventually be offset by decline, leading to predictable exit. In an AI longevity economy, experience compounds without equivalent deterioration, producing workers whose expertise deepens across unusually long arcs. This sustained capability changes how value is created and evaluated. Productivity becomes less age-dependent and more adaptability-dependent. Workers are defined less by chronological stage and more by functional capacity.

Artificial intelligence amplifies this shift by augmenting human cognition and reducing the physical burdens historically associated with aging. Decision-support systems enhance analytical performance, offsetting declines in processing speed. Automation handles repetitive or physically demanding tasks, preserving energy for strategic work. AI-driven collaboration tools enable remote and asynchronous participation, removing geographic and mobility constraints that once limited older workers. The result is an environment where age-related barriers diminish, allowing individuals to contribute meaningfully across extended spans. Work becomes less constrained by biology and more shaped by skill, creativity, and accumulated knowledge.

Career structures inevitably evolve in response. The linear career arc—entry, advancement, plateau, retirement—fragments into multiple phases of reinvention. Individuals may pursue sequential professions, alternating between periods of employment, education, entrepreneurship, and recovery. AI facilitates this multi-phase model by mapping transferable skills, predicting labor demand, and personalizing training pathways. Continuous learning platforms adapt to user performance, enabling rapid acquisition of new competencies regardless of age. The boundary between career stages dissolves. Work becomes cyclical rather than terminal. Extended lifespan transforms careers from finite trajectories into iterative journeys.

This transformation carries significant implications for productivity at both individual and macroeconomic levels. At the individual level, extended productive lifespan allows expertise to mature fully. Many fields—science, medicine, engineering, strategy, creative arts—reward deep knowledge accumulated over decades. Historically, individuals often reached peak mastery near the end of their working lives, only to exit soon after. AI longevity allows this mastery phase to persist, increasing lifetime output. At the societal level, retaining experienced workers preserves institutional knowledge and reduces skill shortages in complex domains. Economies benefit from a larger pool of high-expertise contributors operating simultaneously across age groups.

However, the extended workforce also introduces generational dynamics that require careful management. When older workers remain active longer, opportunities for advancement among younger cohorts may appear constrained. Traditional hierarchical structures assumed predictable turnover as senior roles vacated. Extended participation disrupts this cycle, potentially creating bottlenecks in promotion pathways. Organizations must adapt by expanding lateral mobility, creating project-based leadership roles, and valuing mentorship as productive contribution. AI can support this transition by identifying skill complementarities across age groups and optimizing team composition based on capability rather than tenure. The goal shifts from replacement to integration.

Retirement itself undergoes redefinition within the extended workforce. Rather than a fixed endpoint, retirement becomes a flexible spectrum of reduced intensity, intermittent engagement, or role transition. Individuals may downshift workload while maintaining participation in advisory, creative, or entrepreneurial activities. Financial independence replaces chronological retirement as the determinant of work cessation. AI-driven financial planning integrates healthspan projections and income flexibility, enabling individuals to design phased participation strategies aligned with evolving capacity and preference. Work becomes elective rather than obligatory, yet remains accessible because capability persists.

Labor markets must adapt structurally to harness extended participation. Age discrimination policies, pension eligibility rules, and employment contracts originally designed for shorter careers become misaligned with longevity realities. Governments and institutions face the challenge of creating inclusive frameworks that encourage continued engagement without coercion. Incentives for lifelong learning, flexible employment arrangements, and health maintenance programs become economically rational investments rather than social accommodations. Extended workforce participation increases tax contributions, reduces dependency ratios, and stabilizes public finances in aging societies. Longevity thus transforms older workers from fiscal liabilities into productive assets.

Entrepreneurship plays a particularly important role in the extended workforce. Longer healthy lives allow individuals to accumulate capital, networks, and experience before launching ventures later in life. AI tools dramatically lower operational barriers, enabling individuals to start businesses with minimal infrastructure. This convergence encourages midlife and later-life entrepreneurship, diversifying innovation sources and expanding economic dynamism. Mature entrepreneurs often combine risk awareness with strategic insight, producing resilient ventures. Extended lifespan multiplies opportunities for experimentation, failure, and refinement across decades, increasing the probability of eventual success. Longevity capital expresses itself through sustained entrepreneurial potential.

Education systems must also transform to support extended careers. Front-loaded education models assume limited career duration; extended workforce participation requires continuous reskilling. AI-driven learning environments personalize pace, modality, and content across the lifespan, enabling efficient skill acquisition even in later years. Credentialing systems shift toward modular and stackable certifications rather than singular degrees. Learning integrates with employment cycles, creating adaptive career ecosystems. The distinction between student and worker fades, replaced by lifelong participants in evolving knowledge networks. Education becomes infrastructure for longevity productivity.

Yet the extended workforce introduces ethical considerations alongside opportunity. If longevity technologies and adaptive education remain unevenly distributed, workforce extension may disproportionately benefit already advantaged populations. Highly skilled individuals with access to health optimization and retraining tools remain employable longer, while others face earlier obsolescence. This divergence risks widening economic inequality across both age and class. Inclusive longevity economies must ensure access to health maintenance, continuous learning, and flexible employment across socioeconomic groups. AI can aid by scaling education and preventive health affordably, but policy design determines distribution.

Ultimately, the extended workforce reframes the meaning of aging itself. Age ceases to mark withdrawal and instead denotes accumulated capability. Societies that embrace this shift unlock unprecedented human potential: decades of additional creativity, productivity, and contribution. Individuals gain the freedom to pursue multiple ambitions across extended timelines. Organizations benefit from sustained expertise and intergenerational collaboration. Economies gain resilience from expanded participation. The extended workforce is not merely a consequence of longer life; it is the economic expression of longevity capital applied to human labor. In the AI longevity era, work expands with life, and the productive horizon moves outward with each added healthy year.

Second Spring

Marcus Alvarez had retired at sixty-five with the quiet satisfaction of someone who had fulfilled expectations. He had worked four decades as a civil engineer, raised two children, paid off his home, and contributed steadily to his pension. Retirement, as he understood it, was the earned reward for endurance—a time to rest after productivity had been spent. For the first year, he embraced the rhythm of unstructured days: morning walks, reading, occasional travel. Yet beneath the calm lay an unease he struggled to articulate. His mind remained active, curious, and capable, but the structure that once channeled it into purpose had vanished. He had prepared financially for retirement, but not psychologically for the loss of direction.

At sixty-seven, Marcus attended a community seminar on longevity and work hosted by a local university. He expected general advice about staying active, but the presentation introduced concepts that unsettled his assumptions. AI-driven health assessments suggested that many individuals of his age could remain cognitively and physically capable for decades. Extended lifespan projections indicated that retirement at sixty-five might leave twenty or thirty healthy years unstructured. The presenter posed a question that lingered in

Marcus's thoughts: what if retirement was not the end of contribution, but the beginning of a second productive phase?

Curiosity led him to undergo an AI-based functional capacity evaluation offered through the university's longevity program. The analysis measured strength, endurance, reaction time, memory, and learning speed relative to age-adjusted norms. The results surprised him. His cognitive processing and spatial reasoning remained well above average, consistent with his engineering background. Physical metrics showed mild decline but high recoverability with targeted training. The system projected that with modest intervention he could maintain professional-level cognitive performance for at least fifteen to twenty years. Marcus stared at the report, unsettled not by limitation but by possibility.

The realization did not immediately translate into action. For months he wrestled with internal resistance. His identity had been anchored in the linear arc of career followed by retirement. Re-entering productive life felt like reversing a natural sequence. Yet the sense of unused capacity persisted. Eventually he enrolled in a part-time online certification in sustainable infrastructure design, a field adjacent to his previous work but shaped by modern environmental and AI modeling tools. The adaptive learning platform adjusted pace to his performance, and he discovered that his decades of engineering intuition accelerated his mastery of new concepts. Learning reignited dormant excitement.

As Marcus progressed, he began contributing to collaborative design forums populated by younger engineers. At first he hesitated, aware of his age among peers decades younger. But his practical experience proved invaluable. He could foresee structural challenges others overlooked, suggest cost-efficient alternatives, and contextualize theoretical models with real-world constraints. The community responded with respect rather than condescension. Age, in that digital environment, became invisible compared to capability. Marcus realized that his accumulated expertise, far from obsolete, had become rare.

Encouraged, he accepted a contract role with a small engineering consultancy specializing in climate-resilient infrastructure. The work was flexible, remote, and project-based—well suited to his desired pace. Each assignment drew on both his historical experience and newly acquired sustainability frameworks. He felt again the rhythm of problem-solving that had defined his earlier career. Yet this time the pressure differed. Financial necessity no longer drove him; engagement did. Work had become elective participation in meaningful challenges rather than obligatory employment.

Years passed, and Marcus's second career expanded. He mentored younger engineers, advised municipalities on infrastructure adaptation, and contributed to interdisciplinary panels exploring longevity-aware urban planning. His perspective bridged eras: traditional engineering rigor combined with emerging AI-driven design. Clients valued not only his knowledge but his calm decision-making under uncertainty. Experience had matured into wisdom, and extended lifespan allowed that wisdom to remain active rather than retire prematurely.

Marcus often reflected on the psychological transformation that accompanied his extended workforce participation. Retirement had initially signaled closure, a narrowing of identity. Re-engagement reopened possibility. He no longer divided life into productive and post-productive phases. Instead he perceived continuity—a long arc of evolving contribution. His days regained structure, but without the constraints that once limited them. He chose projects aligned with curiosity and values. Time expanded from something to be filled into something to be shaped.

At seventy-six, Marcus stood at a coastal construction site reviewing plans for a flood-resilient community center. Younger engineers moved around him, tablets in hand, analyzing AI-generated simulations of tidal patterns. Marcus traced structural reinforcements with his finger, suggesting adjustments based on decades of material behavior observation. The team listened closely. He felt neither outdated nor exceptional—simply integrated. His presence represented continuity across generations, knowledge extended rather than replaced. That evening he returned home overlooking the bay and considered the unlikely trajectory of his later years. Had he followed his original retirement model, he might have spent these years in quiet disengagement, his expertise fading unused. Instead he experienced what he privately called his second spring—a season of renewed growth occurring not despite age but enabled by sustained health and opportunity. Longevity had not merely added years; it had restored purpose to years that might otherwise have narrowed.

Marcus realized that extended workforce participation had altered his perception of aging itself. Age was no longer a marker of decline but of accumulation—skills layered, insight deepened, perspective widened. AI tools had facilitated retraining and flexible work structures, but the deeper transformation lay in recognizing that productive capacity can persist when supported. Retirement, he concluded, should never have been defined by age alone. It should be defined by choice.

On his seventy-eighth birthday, Marcus received a message from a former student he had mentored online years earlier. The young engineer, now leading a major sustainability initiative, thanked him for guidance that had shaped her career. Marcus read the note slowly, aware that his influence extended beyond projects into people. Contribution, he realized, multiplies when time extends. His life's work had not ended at sixty-five; it had continued, expanded, and matured across decades he once assumed belonged only to rest.

Standing at his window watching the tide roll in under moonlight, Marcus felt no urgency about remaining years. Whether ten or twenty lay ahead mattered less than the knowledge that each remained open to purpose. Longevity had rewritten the script of his life. Retirement had been an ending imagined by a shorter-lived world. In the extended workforce of the longevity age, his story had simply entered its next chapter.

Chapter 3

The Longevity Dividend: How Extended Healthspan Is Reshaping Healthcare Costs, Productivity, and National Wealth

For decades, aging populations were framed primarily as an economic burden. Policymakers projected rising healthcare costs, expanding pension liabilities, and shrinking labor forces as longevity increased. This narrative assumed that additional years of life would be dominated by chronic disease, disability, and dependency. Artificial intelligence–enabled longevity alters this equation fundamentally by extending healthspan—the portion of life spent in good health—rather than merely prolonging survival. When additional years are lived with vitality and capability, the economic implications reverse. Instead of generating escalating costs, extended healthspan produces a longevity dividend: a compound economic gain derived from sustained productivity, reduced disease burden, and preserved human capital across longer lifespans.

The longevity dividend begins with a simple but powerful shift in cost structure. Traditional healthcare expenditures concentrate heavily in the final years of life, driven by chronic disease management, hospitalization, and long-term care. AI-driven prevention and early detection compress morbidity, delaying the onset of major illness and shortening periods of severe decline. As populations spend more years in high-functioning health states and fewer years in intensive medical need, lifetime healthcare costs may stabilize or even decline despite longer lifespans. This does not eliminate healthcare spending; rather, it redistributes it toward preventive monitoring, personalized intervention, and longitudinal health optimization. Economically, prevention expenditures tend to be lower, more predictable, and more scalable than acute care costs, improving system sustainability.

Extended healthspan simultaneously preserves productivity. Individuals who remain physically and cognitively capable contribute to economic activity across additional decades. This sustained participation increases aggregate labor supply without requiring population growth, particularly valuable in societies experiencing declining birth rates. Experienced workers remain engaged, reducing skill shortages and preserving institutional knowledge. Extended productive years generate additional income, tax contributions, and innovation output. The macroeconomic effect resembles a demographic expansion achieved biologically rather than reproductively.

Nations effectively gain a larger, healthier workforce without increasing population size, enhancing economic resilience.

AI plays a central role in enabling the longevity dividend by transforming healthcare from reactive treatment to predictive maintenance. Machine-learning models analyze biomarkers, lifestyle data, and genetic risk to forecast disease trajectories years before symptoms appear. Continuous monitoring technologies detect subtle physiological changes, enabling early intervention. Personalized treatment plans optimize nutrition, activity, sleep, and medication for individual biology. This shift reduces catastrophic health events such as cardiovascular crises, metabolic collapse, and neurodegenerative progression. Economically, preventing a single severe chronic condition can save years of medical expense and preserve decades of productivity. When scaled across populations, such prevention generates substantial fiscal benefit.

Healthcare labor economics also evolve under extended healthspan. Aging populations traditionally increase demand for intensive care services and long-term caregiving, straining healthcare workforces. If individuals remain healthier longer, the burden shifts toward preventive and outpatient services, which are less resource-intensive. AI-assisted diagnostics and automation further reduce clinician workload by handling routine analysis and monitoring tasks. Healthcare professionals transition from crisis response to health optimization roles. This reallocation improves efficiency and mitigates workforce shortages, particularly in geriatric and chronic care sectors. The system spends more effort maintaining wellness and less effort managing decline.

The longevity dividend extends beyond healthcare into social systems. Pension and social security programs were designed when retirement periods were relatively short. Extended healthspan allows individuals to remain economically active longer, delaying benefit claims and increasing contribution periods. This improves the ratio of contributors to beneficiaries, strengthening fiscal stability. Even modest increases in average retirement age, aligned with improved healthspan, significantly reduce pension system strain. AI-enabled financial and health forecasting allows individuals and governments to align retirement timing with functional capacity rather than chronological age. Longevity thus transforms aging populations from fiscal liabilities into balanced participants in economic cycles.

Human capital preservation represents another dimension of the longevity dividend. Skills, expertise, and institutional memory accumulate over decades but were historically lost as individuals aged out of participation. Extended healthspan retains this capital within economies longer, enhancing innovation and strategic capacity. Experienced professionals contribute mentorship, leadership, and knowledge transfer across generations. Industries with long learning curves—medicine, engineering, research, governance—benefit particularly from sustained expertise. The economic value of retained human capital often exceeds direct productivity, influencing decision quality and organizational stability. Longevity amplifies the return on educational investment across a longer horizon.

At the macroeconomic level, extended healthspan influences consumption patterns and market dynamics. Healthy older adults remain active consumers across sectors including travel, education, technology, housing, and wellness services. Rather than shifting spending toward healthcare alone, longevity diversifies demand. New industries emerge around midlife education, preventive health technology, adaptive housing, and longevity lifestyle services. Economic activity expands in response to sustained engagement across age groups. Markets evolve to serve populations whose needs change gradually rather than abruptly with age. Longevity thus generates not only cost savings but new revenue streams and employment sectors.

However, realizing the longevity dividend depends on equitable distribution of healthspan gains. If longevity technologies remain concentrated among affluent populations, economic benefits will accrue unevenly. Societies may experience dual aging trajectories: one population segment remaining healthy and productive, another facing traditional decline. Such divergence undermines aggregate economic gains and intensifies inequality. Inclusive access to preventive healthcare, AI diagnostics, and lifestyle optimization becomes essential for maximizing national longevity dividends. Public health infrastructure and policy incentives must support broad adoption rather than niche optimization. Longevity economics is inherently population-based; its dividend scales with inclusivity.

Measuring the longevity dividend requires new economic metrics. Traditional indicators such as life expectancy fail to capture functional health and productivity. Health-adjusted life expectancy, functional capacity indices, and lifetime productivity measures better reflect economic impact. AI enables continuous population health analytics, allowing policymakers to track healthspan distribution and intervention effectiveness. These metrics inform investment decisions across healthcare, education, and labor policy. Nations capable of quantifying longevity capital can strategically allocate resources to maximize long-term returns. Health becomes measurable infrastructure contributing directly to economic output.

Yet the longevity dividend is not automatic. Without proactive investment in preventive systems and adaptive institutions, extended lifespan alone may still increase costs. AI-enabled longevity must be integrated into healthcare delivery, education, labor markets, and retirement frameworks to translate biological gains into economic value. Policy inertia risks lagging behind technological progress, delaying benefits and exacerbating disparities. The longevity dividend emerges when societies align systems with extended healthspan reality—shifting from treating aging as decline to managing aging as sustained capability.

Ultimately, the longevity dividend reframes the economics of aging. Longer healthy lives generate compound returns: reduced disease burden, extended productivity, preserved human capital, diversified consumption, and stabilized social systems. AI serves as both catalyst and optimizer, enabling prevention and extending capability. Nations and individuals that invest early in healthspan expansion capture disproportionate benefits. Aging ceases to represent inevitable economic drag and instead becomes a source of growth. The longevity dividend represents one of the most profound economic opportunities of the AI age: the conversion of added years into sustained human value.

The Years That Returned

Dr. Leena Shah had spent most of her career confronting the costs of aging. As a public health physician working in urban hospitals, she witnessed the same pattern repeatedly: patients arriving late in life burdened by decades of unmanaged chronic disease. Diabetes, heart failure, cognitive decline, mobility impairment—conditions layered until independence dissolved. Treatment often stabilized but rarely restored. Leena came to associate aging with narrowing possibilities, where each year added complexity and expense rather than vitality. The healthcare system, she believed, was built to manage deterioration rather than sustain health.

In her early fifties, Leena joined a research initiative exploring AI-driven preventive health programs across community populations. The project deployed wearable monitoring, metabolic screening, and personalized lifestyle coaching guided by predictive algorithms. Participants received continuous feedback on nutrition, activity, sleep, and cardiovascular metrics. The goal was simple yet ambitious: delay disease onset across midlife populations. Leena approached the work analytically, expecting modest statistical improvements rather than transformative change.

The first data surprised her. Within two years, participants exhibited measurable reductions in metabolic risk markers, improved cardiovascular fitness, and decreased incidence of early-stage diabetes. Hospital admissions among the cohort declined significantly compared to control populations. But numbers alone did not convey the shift Leena observed in clinic visits. Patients previously resigned to gradual decline arrived reporting increased energy, restored mobility, and renewed engagement in work and family roles. They were not merely living longer; they were living differently.

One patient in particular altered Leena's perspective. Miguel Torres, a fifty-eight-year-old bus driver, had entered the program with hypertension, obesity, and prediabetes. His work schedule and financial constraints had long limited healthcare engagement. The AI-guided system delivered personalized interventions compatible with his routine: short exercise intervals during route breaks, targeted nutrition adjustments using affordable foods, and sleep optimization strategies for shift work. Over three years, Miguel lost weight, normalized glucose levels, and improved cardiovascular capacity. More importantly, he regained stamina and mental clarity he had not experienced since his thirties.

During a follow-up visit, Miguel spoke with quiet conviction. "I thought my best years were over," he told Leena. "Now I feel like they came back." He had enrolled in evening technical courses, planning to transition into transportation logistics management. His renewed health expanded his sense of future. Leena realized that the program had not only prevented disease; it had restored possibility. Miguel's productive horizon extended beyond what he once assumed. Healthspan had returned years he believed lost.

As the study progressed, similar stories accumulated. Participants delayed retirement, pursued new careers, or increased community involvement. Healthcare utilization shifted from emergency interventions to preventive check-ins. Leena began analyzing economic outcomes alongside medical data. Reduced hospitalization costs combined with sustained employment and tax contribution produced measurable fiscal benefit. The cohort generated what economists termed a longevity dividend—economic gains derived from preserved health and productivity. Leena saw the abstraction embodied in individual lives.

Her professional focus transformed. She transitioned from hospital-based care to designing community longevity programs integrating AI monitoring, behavioral coaching, and accessible preventive services. The goal expanded from treating illness to extending healthy years across populations. Funding agencies initially hesitated, accustomed to disease-focused metrics. Leena reframed proposals around economic returns: reduced healthcare expenditure, increased workforce participation, and preserved human capital. Gradually policymakers recognized the broader impact. Longevity programs scaled across districts. Years later, Leena visited Miguel at his new workplace overseeing transportation logistics systems. He greeted her with energetic confidence. At sixty-eight, he remained active, cognitively sharp, and professionally engaged. He described mentoring younger staff and pursuing advanced certifications. "I didn't retire," he said with a smile. "I upgraded." Leena felt the phrase capture the essence of longevity economics: extended health enabling extended contribution. Miguel's life illustrated the years that returned—not simply added time but restored capacity.

Leena herself experienced the shift personally. Immersed in preventive health research, she adopted the same monitoring and optimization strategies promoted in her programs. Her stamina increased, concentration deepened, and recovery from stress improved. She noticed that her professional ambition extended beyond traditional midlife expectations. Rather than contemplating gradual reduction of workload, she envisioned decades of continued innovation in public health systems. Longevity reshaped her own horizon.

At sixty-five, instead of retiring from clinical leadership, Leena assumed a national advisory role shaping preventive health policy. Her expertise, matured across decades, guided large-scale implementation of AI-driven longevity programs. Hospitalization rates declined nationally in participating regions, while workforce participation among older adults rose. The longevity dividend materialized not only in statistics but in lived experience across communities. Aging populations no longer appeared solely as cost centers but as sustained contributors.

One evening after a policy summit, Leena walked through a city park filled with people of varied ages exercising, learning, and socializing. She noticed older adults jogging beside younger ones, community classes blending generations, and health kiosks offering real-time monitoring. The environment reflected structural change: societies adapting to extended healthspan. She thought of her earlier career surrounded by late-stage disease and realized how profoundly expectations had shifted. Aging had not disappeared; decline still occurred. But the boundary between vitality and illness had moved outward, returning years once assumed lost.

Leena paused near a bench where an older man guided a child through mathematics exercises on a tablet. The scene symbolized continuity across time—experience mentoring youth, capacity persisting across age. She felt a quiet satisfaction knowing her work contributed to such moments. The longevity dividend was not abstract fiscal gain; it was reclaimed life potential distributed across society. Years returned to individuals became value returned to communities. As twilight settled, Leena reflected on her own trajectory. She had begun her career managing the costs of aging. She now shaped systems that expanded its possibilities. AI had enabled prevention and extended healthspan, but the deeper transformation lay in redefining expectations of later life. Additional years no longer signified inevitable decline; they represented renewed opportunity for contribution. The years that returned altered both individual lives and collective prosperity.

Walking home, Leena felt neither older nor younger—only extended. Time ahead remained open, shaped by sustained health and purpose. The longevity dividend, she understood, was ultimately human: the conversion of added years into continued meaning.

Chapter 4

The New Retirement Equation: How AI, Longevity, and Extended Healthspan Are Redefining Retirement, Savings, and Financial Independence

For most of modern economic history, retirement was treated as a predictable life stage defined by chronological age rather than functional capacity. Financial systems assumed a relatively short post-work lifespan, typically one or two decades, during which accumulated savings and pensions would sustain individuals no longer engaged in labor. Artificial intelligence–enabled longevity disrupts this assumption fundamentally. As healthspan extends and individuals remain capable of productive engagement far beyond traditional retirement age, the economic logic of retirement must be recalculated. Retirement transitions from a fixed endpoint into a dynamic equation balancing health, capability, financial independence, and personal choice across extended lifespans.

The traditional retirement model relies on three premises: that earning capacity declines sharply with age, that healthcare costs rise steeply in later years, and that lifespan after workforce exit remains limited. AI longevity alters each premise simultaneously. Sustained cognitive and physical function allows continued earning potential across additional decades. Preventive health optimization delays severe medical costs. Lifespan projections extend well beyond historical expectations. When individuals may remain capable into their seventies or eighties, retiring permanently at sixty-five creates a prolonged period of financial dependency unsupported by original system design. The retirement equation must therefore incorporate longevity capital: the capacity to generate income, adapt skills, and maintain productivity across extended time horizons.

Financial planning models historically concentrated wealth accumulation into a compressed midlife earning window followed by a withdrawal phase. Extended healthspan expands the earning window itself. Individuals may accumulate assets across fifty or sixty productive years rather than thirty. Compounding over extended duration dramatically increases potential wealth, even with moderate income levels. Conversely, premature retirement in an extended-lifespan world amplifies financial risk, as savings must sustain longer non-earning periods. AI-driven financial planning integrates healthspan forecasts, career adaptability projections, and lifespan probabilities to optimize contribution and withdrawal strategies dynamically. Retirement becomes a personalized trajectory rather than a standardized age threshold.

AI transforms retirement planning through predictive analytics. Longevity models estimate individual healthspan based on biomarkers, lifestyle, genetics, and behavior patterns. Career adaptability algorithms assess potential for continued skill relevance. Financial simulations integrate these variables with investment performance and consumption patterns. The result is a probabilistic retirement horizon reflecting functional capacity rather than chronological age. Individuals can visualize scenarios: continued part-time work extending asset growth, phased retirement balancing income and leisure, or entrepreneurial engagement replacing traditional employment. AI shifts retirement planning from static projection to adaptive strategy aligned with evolving health and opportunity.

The concept of financial independence evolves accordingly. In traditional frameworks, financial independence implied complete detachment from labor income. In longevity economies, independence increasingly reflects optionality—the freedom to choose work intensity rather than cease work entirely. Extended healthspan allows individuals to pursue meaningful engagement without financial necessity. Income may derive from advisory roles, creative ventures, mentorship, or flexible consulting. This diversified income profile reduces reliance on savings depletion and prolongs asset longevity. Retirement thus becomes a spectrum of engagement calibrated to personal preference and capability rather than binary employment status.

Pension and social security systems face profound recalibration under extended longevity. These programs were designed when retirement durations were shorter and contributor-to-beneficiary ratios higher. Extended healthspan offers an opportunity to stabilize such systems by aligning eligibility with functional capacity rather than fixed age. Gradual retirement age adjustments reflecting population health improvements can significantly reduce fiscal strain. AI-enabled demographic modeling allows governments to forecast healthspan distribution and calibrate benefit structures accordingly. Flexible claiming options encourage continued participation while preserving individual choice. Longevity economics transforms retirement policy from age-based entitlement toward capability-based support.

Healthcare costs, central to retirement planning, also shift under extended healthspan. Traditional projections anticipated escalating medical expenses in late life, necessitating substantial retirement reserves. AI-driven preventive health compresses morbidity, reducing duration of intensive care periods. While preventive and monitoring costs persist, catastrophic expenditures decline or occur later. Financial planning can therefore allocate resources differently, emphasizing long-term health maintenance rather than acute care buffers. Insurance products evolve to reflect healthspan trajectories, integrating wellness incentives and dynamic premiums. Retirement planning incorporates health optimization as financial strategy, recognizing that sustained vitality preserves both income potential and asset value.

Labor markets respond to changing retirement patterns by expanding flexible employment structures. Part-time roles, project-based contracts, advisory positions, and remote participation allow older individuals to remain economically active without full-time commitments. AI platforms match experienced professionals with organizations seeking specialized knowledge, facilitating late-career engagement. Employers benefit from retained expertise without long-term employment liabilities. Workers benefit from income continuity and purpose. The retirement boundary blurs into adaptive participation. Longevity capital remains economically engaged rather than withdrawn abruptly.

Wealth transfer dynamics also transform under extended lifespans. Traditional inheritance models assumed relatively early intergenerational transfer as parents aged. Longer healthy lives delay wealth transfer, extending financial autonomy of older generations. Families may span five or six living generations simultaneously, complicating asset distribution and dependency structures. Extended accumulation periods increase total wealth before transfer but postpone its availability to younger cohorts. AI-assisted estate planning adapts to these dynamics by modeling multi-generational timelines and optimizing transfer strategies across extended horizons. Retirement economics thus intersects with family economics in unprecedented ways.

Psychological dimensions of retirement evolve alongside financial structures. Historically, retirement symbolized cessation of productive identity. Extended healthspan undermines this narrative by preserving capability. Individuals increasingly view later life as a phase of reinvention rather than withdrawal. Continuous learning, entrepreneurship, and creative pursuits become viable decades beyond traditional retirement age. AI learning platforms and collaborative networks support this transition. Economic engagement aligns with personal fulfillment rather than necessity alone. Retirement identity shifts from rest after labor to freedom within extended capability.

Yet the new retirement equation introduces equity challenges. Individuals with access to longevity-enhancing healthcare and adaptive education can extend earning capacity, while others remain constrained by traditional health decline. Unequal longevity capital risks producing retirement disparities where some enjoy decades of optional engagement and others face premature incapacity. Inclusive longevity economies must ensure access to preventive health, reskilling opportunities, and flexible employment across socioeconomic groups. Policy design determines whether extended retirement horizons become universal benefit or concentrated privilege. Longevity economics requires distributional fairness to sustain legitimacy.

Ultimately, the new retirement equation integrates four variables: healthspan, capability, financial assets, and choice. AI enables measurement and optimization of each. Retirement ceases to be defined by age alone and instead reflects the intersection of sustained health and financial independence. Individuals may transition gradually from full-time work to partial engagement to elective contribution across extended timelines. Societies adapt by redesigning pension systems, labor markets, and financial planning frameworks to accommodate longevity realities. Retirement transforms from an endpoint into a flexible phase within longer, healthier lives. In the AI longevity era, the true goal is not retirement from life but freedom within extended living.

The Longest Freedom

When Helen Carter retired at sixty-four, she believed she had reached the destination she had worked toward for decades.

Her career as a public school principal had demanded relentless attention—budgets, staffing, student crises, community pressures. Retirement promised relief. She envisioned quiet mornings, travel with her husband, and time finally her own. For the first year, the plan unfolded as expected. She rested, visited friends, and explored hobbies postponed by professional demands. Yet gradually a subtle restlessness emerged. Her energy remained strong, her mind alert, and her sense of purpose unfulfilled. Retirement felt less like liberation and more like suspension.

At sixty-six, Helen attended a financial wellness seminar organized by her pension fund. The session introduced updated longevity projections indicating that many retirees might live into their nineties with sustained health. The presenter emphasized that retirement periods now often spanned thirty years or more. Helen realized that her financial planning had assumed far shorter horizons. More unsettling was the recognition that her personal horizon—her capacity for engagement—remained wide. She did not feel finished. She felt paused.

Curiosity led her to explore part-time educational consulting opportunities. AI-based professional networks matched experienced educators with schools seeking strategic guidance. Helen accepted a short-term advisory role assisting a rural district implementing digital learning programs. The work was remote, flexible, and intellectually stimulating. Within weeks she felt familiar engagement returning—the satisfaction of problem-solving, mentoring staff, and shaping outcomes. Retirement, she discovered, need not exclude contribution.

The experience shifted her perception of freedom. Previously she had equated freedom with absence of responsibility. Now she saw freedom as choice over engagement. She could accept projects aligned with her values and decline those that did not. Income from consulting supplemented her pension, extending financial security. More importantly, purpose returned. Helen's days regained structure without constraint. She was neither fully retired nor fully employed; she occupied a new space between, shaped by extended capability.

Over the next decade Helen's role evolved. She specialized in mentoring first-time school leaders navigating complex administrative demands. Her decades of experience allowed her to anticipate challenges others encountered for the first time. Schools across regions sought her guidance. She traveled occasionally but worked primarily from home, balancing professional engagement with personal life. Her income became diversified—pension, consulting, speaking engagements—reducing reliance on savings withdrawal. Financial independence transformed from static retirement to dynamic participation. Helen noticed parallel changes among peers. Friends once fully retired began exploring phased engagement—teaching short courses, advising nonprofits, launching small ventures. Extended healthspan allowed sustained activity without exhaustion. The shared narrative shifted from "retired" to "independent." They worked by choice, not necessity. The boundary between working years and retirement years blurred into continuity. Helen realized her generation stood at the threshold of a new retirement paradigm.

At seventy-eight Helen's husband passed away after a brief illness. The loss was profound, but her continued engagement provided structure during grief. Consulting projects connected her with communities and purpose beyond personal sorrow. She recognized that extended participation had not only economic value but emotional resilience. Retirement as complete withdrawal might have intensified isolation. Instead, optional work sustained connection and meaning. Longevity freedom included psychological stability.

Years later Helen's consulting network expanded internationally through AI collaboration platforms translating expertise across languages and educational systems. She mentored school leaders in regions she had never visited physically. Age mattered little in digital exchange; insight traveled independent of geography. Her influence extended further in later life than during full-time employment. Retirement had not diminished impact; it had reconfigured it.

On her eighty-fifth birthday Helen received a letter from a young principal she had mentored years earlier. The educator described how Helen's guidance during a difficult transition had preserved a struggling school and inspired long-term reforms. Reading the letter, Helen realized that her later-life contributions had shaped institutions and individuals beyond her earlier career. Extended years had multiplied influence. Longevity had transformed retirement into expansion rather than contraction.

Sitting on her porch that evening, Helen reflected on the unexpected arc of her later life. She had once viewed retirement as the final chapter—a deserved rest after service. Instead it had become the longest freedom: decades of self-directed engagement enabled by sustained health and financial independence. She had chosen projects, schedules, and causes aligned with personal meaning. Work no longer defined identity; choice did. Longevity had extended both time and autonomy.

As twilight settled, Helen considered what freedom truly meant. Not the absence of activity, but the presence of possibility. Retirement had ceased to be withdrawal from contribution and instead became liberation from compulsion. She had worked because she wished to, not because she must. Financial security combined with enduring capability allowed participation without pressure. This, she realized, was the new retirement equation lived personally.

Helen rose and walked inside, reviewing the next month's mentorship schedule. Even at eighty-five she anticipated conversations, challenges, and growth. Years ahead remained open, not empty. Longevity had rewritten the script she once inherited from shorter-lived generations. Retirement had not ended her work; it had transformed it into freedom.

Chapter 5

Lifespan Inequality: How Unequal Access to Longevity Technologies Could Redefine Wealth, Opportunity, and Social Mobility

Throughout history, inequality has been measured primarily in material terms—income, assets, education, and access to opportunity. Longevity has varied across populations, but differences in lifespan were typically interpreted as public health disparities rather than structural economic divisions. Artificial intelligence–enabled longevity introduces a new dimension of inequality that is both biological and economic: lifespan inequality. As AI-driven preventive healthcare, health optimization technologies, and cognitive enhancement tools extend healthy years disproportionately among populations with greater resources and access, longevity itself becomes a stratified asset. Time—specifically healthy, productive time—emerges as a determinant of wealth and opportunity as powerful as capital or education.

Lifespan inequality arises from differential access to healthspan-extending systems. Advanced diagnostics, personalized prevention platforms, genetic screening, continuous monitoring devices, and AI-guided lifestyle optimization programs initially concentrate in affluent healthcare markets. Individuals able to adopt these technologies earlier delay disease onset, maintain cognitive function longer, and preserve physical capability. The result is an expanded productive lifespan compared with populations lacking such access. Over decades, these differences accumulate into divergent economic trajectories. Those with extended healthspan retain earning capacity, accumulate assets longer, and sustain participation in knowledge economies, while others face earlier workforce exit and increased healthcare burden. The gap is measured not only in wealth but in years of capability.

This divergence compounds across generations. Families benefiting from extended healthspan preserve human capital longer, transferring not only financial resources but sustained mentorship and stability to younger members. Parents and grandparents remain economically and cognitively active, supporting education and opportunity across extended timelines. In contrast, families experiencing shorter healthspans may confront early illness, income disruption, and caregiving burdens that constrain advancement. Lifespan inequality thus reinforces intergenerational inequality. Longevity becomes inherited advantage, mediated by access to health optimization infrastructure rather than genetics alone.

AI accelerates this process by amplifying the returns to early adoption. Preventive systems are most effective when implemented before disease onset, often decades before symptoms emerge. Populations with routine access to screening and monitoring benefit from earlier intervention and compounding health gains. AI-driven health models improve continuously with data input, further enhancing outcomes for participants while leaving non-participants behind. The feedback loop resembles technological network effects: the more individuals engage with longevity systems, the more effective they become. Lifespan inequality widens not linearly but exponentially over time.

Economic consequences extend into labor markets. Individuals with extended healthspan remain employable longer, retaining income streams and professional relevance. They can retrain, pivot careers, and pursue entrepreneurship across extended timelines. Those with constrained healthspan face earlier decline in productivity and higher medical costs, limiting economic participation. Workforce extension becomes a privilege correlated with access to longevity capital. Employers increasingly favor workers able to maintain performance across long arcs, reinforcing advantages for longevity-optimized populations. Economic mobility becomes tied to biological durability. Healthcare financing structures may unintentionally reinforce lifespan inequality. Systems emphasizing individualized optimization services, subscription-based preventive platforms, and personalized medicine risk excluding lower-income populations. Without universal preventive access, healthcare remains reactive for disadvantaged groups and proactive for advantaged ones. The divergence in disease onset age translates into divergent lifetime medical cost burdens and productivity loss. Lifespan inequality thus emerges partly from systemic design rather than inherent biological difference. Policy choices determine whether longevity technologies become public goods or private luxuries.

Education intersects with lifespan inequality through cognitive longevity. AI-driven learning tools and neuroadaptive technologies can preserve learning speed and memory across extended years. Individuals with access maintain skill relevance and adaptability, enabling prolonged participation in evolving labor markets. Others may experience earlier cognitive decline or reduced retraining opportunity, constraining career longevity. Knowledge economies reward sustained cognitive capacity, so disparities in cognitive healthspan translate directly into income inequality. Lifespan inequality thus encompasses both physical and intellectual dimensions.

Geography further shapes longevity distribution. Regions with advanced healthcare infrastructure, preventive public health systems, and digital access adopt AI longevity earlier. Populations in underserved areas may lack basic preventive services, let alone advanced optimization. The global distribution of healthy lifespan diverges accordingly, affecting national productivity and economic competitiveness. Countries investing in population healthspan expansion gain workforce extension and reduced healthcare burden, while others confront persistent disease costs. Longevity inequality thus manifests at both individual and national scales.

Addressing lifespan inequality requires reconceptualizing longevity technologies as societal infrastructure rather than optional consumer products. Preventive healthcare access, AI diagnostics, and health optimization programs must scale broadly to maximize economic benefit and equity. Public health initiatives integrating AI monitoring, community-based interventions, and accessible lifestyle programs can narrow disparities. Insurance and policy frameworks incentivizing prevention rather than treatment align financial incentives with longevity equity. The longevity dividend described earlier depends on inclusivity; unequal distribution undermines aggregate gains.

Ethical considerations emerge as lifespan becomes economically valuable. If extended healthspan correlates with wealth accumulation, societies risk stratification not only by income but by years lived capable. Opportunities for education, career progression, and influence concentrate among those with longer productive horizons. Political representation and leadership may skew toward longevity-advantaged populations. Social mobility could decline if early-life disadvantages shorten healthspan. Ensuring fairness requires intentional distribution of longevity resources and monitoring of lifespan disparities alongside economic indicators.

AI itself can serve as equalizer when deployed inclusively. Low-cost monitoring devices, scalable digital health coaching, and predictive screening accessible through public systems can extend preventive care broadly. Community-based AI health programs have demonstrated ability to reduce chronic disease risk across diverse populations when designed for accessibility. Data-driven public health policy allows targeted intervention where lifespan disparities are greatest. The same technologies that create longevity advantages for some can extend them to many if integrated into equitable frameworks. Distribution, not innovation alone, determines outcome.

Ultimately, lifespan inequality reframes economic justice in the age of longevity. Wealth and opportunity are no longer shaped solely by education or capital but by access to healthy years themselves. Societies must decide whether extended lifespan becomes a universal human advancement or a stratified privilege. Economic systems that distribute longevity capital broadly unlock greater productivity, stability, and cohesion. Those that allow concentration risk deepening divides measured in decades of life. In the AI longevity era, equality increasingly means equal access to time—the foundational resource from which all other forms of wealth emerge.

Equal Years

Jamal Carter grew up in a neighborhood where aging seemed to arrive early. His grandparents moved slowly in their fifties, burdened by hypertension and diabetes common across the community. Many adults left work before sixty due to health decline. Jamal internalized an unspoken expectation: life would narrow sooner rather than later. Ambition existed, but it carried an undertone of urgency, as though time available for achievement was limited. He pursued education diligently, becoming a community organizer focused on economic opportunity, yet the shadow of shortened healthspan lingered.

In his early forties Jamal helped coordinate a pilot public health initiative introducing AI-driven preventive care to underserved districts. Participants received wearable health monitors, nutrition guidance adapted to local food access, and continuous coaching through mobile platforms. The program aimed to reduce chronic disease disparities. Jamal joined primarily as facilitator rather than beneficiary, viewing longevity as a systemic issue rather than personal possibility.

After months observing outcomes, he noticed subtle changes among participants. Neighbors reported improved energy, weight reduction, and stabilized blood pressure. Community walking groups formed spontaneously. Health data visualizations displayed gradual risk decline across the cohort. Jamal realized that preventive tools were altering trajectories previously assumed fixed. Encouraged by colleagues, he enrolled personally in the program, curious about his own baseline metrics.

The initial assessment revealed elevated metabolic risk and early cardiovascular markers common in his demographic group. Yet projections showed high reversibility with targeted intervention. Jamal followed recommendations—structured activity integrated into daily routines, dietary adjustments compatible with neighborhood resources, stress regulation practices. Within a year his markers improved significantly.

He experienced physical stamina he had not felt since youth. More striking was the psychological shift: he began imagining a longer healthy future than he had ever assumed.

This expanded horizon influenced his work. Jamal reframed community development strategies to include longevity equity alongside economic equity. He advocated for preventive health infrastructure as foundational to opportunity. His presentations argued that unequal healthspan limited educational attainment, workforce participation, and wealth accumulation. Extending healthy years across communities, he insisted, was economic justice. Data from pilot programs supported his case. Local governments began funding expansion.

As programs scaled, Jamal observed generational change. Older adults remained active longer, mentoring youth and sustaining employment. Families experienced fewer medical crises and income disruptions. Children saw elders modeling vitality rather than decline. Community expectations shifted from inevitability of early illness to possibility of sustained health. Jamal realized that longevity equity altered not only outcomes but culture. Time horizons expanded collectively.

Personally, Jamal pursued new education in public health policy during his late forties, enabled by restored energy and confidence in extended capability. He transitioned from local organizer to regional strategist coordinating longevity equity initiatives. His career arc lengthened beyond earlier assumptions. Where he once felt urgency to achieve quickly before decline, he now planned across decades. Time had become available resource rather than constraint.

At fifty-eight Jamal visited his childhood neighborhood park, now hosting intergenerational fitness and education programs established through the longevity initiative. He watched older adults exercising alongside younger residents, health monitors tracking progress. The scene contrasted sharply with memories of premature aging he carried from youth. He felt the weight of generational change: years once lost returning to communities historically deprived of them. Longevity was becoming shared rather than stratified.

Years later Jamal's parents, participants in early program phases, remained healthy and active into their seventies. They traveled, volunteered, and supported grandchildren's education. The family timeline expanded beyond Jamal's childhood expectations. He recognized that equalizing access to preventive health had extended not only individual years but familial stability. Lifespan equity translated into opportunity equity across generations.

Standing before an international conference at sixty-five, Jamal summarized decades of work: "We often measure inequality in money or education," he said. "But the deepest inequality is time. When some communities lose healthy years, they lose chances—to learn, to earn, to build. When we restore those years, we restore possibility." The audience, policymakers from diverse nations, recognized the truth in lived evidence. Longevity equity was not charity; it was economic foundation.

After the conference Jamal walked along a river near the venue city, reflecting on his own trajectory. He had once expected narrowing horizons by midlife. Instead he stood vigorous and engaged, planning future initiatives. Preventive systems had altered his biological course, and with it his economic and personal possibilities. He understood intimately that lifespan inequality could be reversed through inclusive design. His life embodied the years returned not only to individuals but to communities.

As evening light shimmered on the water, Jamal considered the meaning of equality in the longevity age. Not identical wealth or status, but equal access to healthy years from which all else could grow. His work continued, driven by the conviction that time itself must be shared. In extending longevity across communities, he had helped equalize the most fundamental currency of human life: the years available to become.

Chapter 6

The 100-Year Career: How AI Longevity Is Transforming Education, Skill Cycles, and Lifelong Earning Potential

For most of modern history, human careers were constrained by biological lifespan and predictable cognitive aging patterns. Education occurred primarily in youth, skill mastery in early adulthood, peak productivity in midlife, and gradual obsolescence thereafter. This sequence shaped educational systems, labor markets, and financial planning structures worldwide. Artificial intelligence–enabled longevity disrupts this temporal architecture by extending both cognitive healthspan and adaptive learning capacity across far longer durations. As individuals remain capable of acquiring new skills and sustaining expertise into later decades, careers evolve from finite arcs into century-scale trajectories. The concept of the 100-year career emerges—not necessarily as continuous employment, but as a prolonged cycle of learning, reinvention, and value creation across extended lifespans.

The traditional education-career-retirement model assumed that knowledge acquired early would sustain decades of work. Yet rapid technological change already shortened skill relevance cycles, requiring periodic retraining even within shorter careers. AI longevity magnifies this need while simultaneously enabling the capacity to meet it. Neurocognitive health preservation, continuous learning platforms, and adaptive education technologies maintain learning speed and memory well into later life. Individuals can therefore re-enter education repeatedly across decades, acquiring new competencies aligned with evolving industries. Education shifts from front-loaded investment to lifelong infrastructure supporting extended productivity.

AI-driven learning environments are central to the 100-year career paradigm. Personalized curricula adapt to cognitive profile, prior knowledge, and learning pace regardless of age. Simulation-based training accelerates mastery by replicating real-world scenarios. Continuous assessment identifies skill gaps and recommends targeted modules. This adaptive system reduces the cognitive friction traditionally associated with late-life learning, enabling efficient reskilling. Economically, the cost-benefit ratio of education improves dramatically when skills can be applied across extended productive years. Training investments yield returns over decades rather than years, encouraging both individuals and institutions to prioritize lifelong education. Career cycles lengthen and multiply under extended longevity. Rather than a single professional identity, individuals may experience several sequential careers separated by phases of education, caregiving, exploration, or recovery. AI labor analytics map transferable skills across industries, facilitating transitions without restarting from zero. Experience accumulated in earlier careers becomes foundation for later specialization rather than barrier to entry. The 100-year career thus resembles a portfolio of evolving roles rather than a ladder culminating in retirement. Economic resilience increases as individuals diversify income sources and adapt to shifting labor demand across extended timelines.

Entrepreneurship becomes increasingly compatible with later-life stages in this framework. Extended healthspan provides time for experimentation and iterative learning across decades. AI tools reduce operational complexity, allowing individuals to launch ventures without extensive physical infrastructure or large teams. Mature professionals leverage accumulated expertise and networks to identify opportunities younger entrepreneurs may overlook. The probability of eventual entrepreneurial success increases when individuals can attempt multiple ventures across extended careers. The 100-year career therefore integrates employment and entrepreneurship fluidly, with transitions guided by opportunity rather than age.

Financial implications of the 100-year career are profound. Extended earning potential allows wealth accumulation across longer periods, reducing pressure on early-life income peaks. Individuals can recover from career disruptions through later reinvention, mitigating long-term financial loss. Retirement savings strategies adjust to phased income patterns rather than abrupt cessation. AI financial planning integrates projected career cycles, healthspan forecasts, and education investments to optimize lifetime earnings. Economic stability improves as income sources diversify temporally and structurally across extended careers.

Labor markets adapt structurally to support century-scale participation. Employers increasingly value learning agility and cross-domain experience rather than static credentials. Hiring practices shift toward skill portfolios and demonstrated adaptability. Career progression becomes nonlinear, accommodating lateral transitions and re-entry after education phases. Age norms in employment erode as capability replaces chronology as performance predictor. Organizations benefit from retaining experienced workers who continuously update skills rather than replacing them prematurely. Workforce participation spans broader age ranges, enhancing diversity of perspective and institutional memory.

The 100-year career also reshapes societal attitudes toward aging and achievement. Traditional milestones—first career, peak position, retirement—lose fixed temporal anchors. Individuals may pursue major professional transformation at ages previously considered late. Lifelong potential expands psychological horizons, encouraging ambition beyond early adulthood. This shift counters age-based stereotypes and unlocks human capital previously constrained by expectations. AI longevity thus not only extends capability but alters cultural narratives about possibility across age.

However, access to lifelong education and cognitive health preservation remains uneven, risking stratification within the 100-year career economy. Individuals with resources can sustain learning and reinvention across decades, while others may face earlier obsolescence due to health decline or limited retraining opportunity. Without inclusive education infrastructure, extended careers may become privilege rather than norm. Public investment in accessible lifelong learning, health maintenance, and career transition support is essential to ensure equitable participation. Longevity economics intersects with education policy to determine whether century-scale careers are widely attainable.

The psychological dimension of the 100-year career also requires adaptation. Extended timelines demand sustained motivation and identity flexibility. Individuals must navigate repeated reinvention without perceiving change as failure. AI career guidance tools support this process by mapping strengths, interests, and opportunities across life stages. Continuous feedback reinforces learning progress and adaptability. Societies that normalize multiple career phases reduce stigma around transition and encourage lifelong development. The 100-year career thrives in cultures valuing growth across age rather than early specialization alone.

Ultimately, the 100-year career represents the economic embodiment of extended lifespan and cognitive longevity. AI enables preservation of learning capacity and accelerates skill acquisition, allowing individuals to create value across unprecedented durations. Education becomes continuous, careers become iterative, and earning potential extends across decades once inaccessible. Individuals gain resilience and opportunity through repeated reinvention. Economies benefit from sustained human capital and adaptive labor forces. In the AI longevity era, a career is no longer a single path traversed once but a long landscape explored repeatedly across a lifetime approaching a century.

Many Lives in One

Sophia Mendes had already lived what most would consider a full professional life by the time she turned fifty-five. She had begun as a journalist, covering social issues across cities and countries, then transitioned into communications leadership for international nonprofits. Her work spanned decades of deadlines, travel, and public campaigns. By her mid-fifties she felt both accomplished and fatigued. Younger colleagues dominated emerging digital media landscapes, and technological shifts seemed to outpace her expertise. She assumed she was approaching the natural closing of her career arc.

Yet Sophia's health told a different story. Years of active living and preventive healthcare left her energetic and mentally sharp. Friends her age spoke of retirement planning, but Sophia felt no internal readiness for withdrawal. Still, she sensed her existing professional identity losing relevance. She faced a question she had never imagined confronting at this stage: what comes next when capability remains but direction fades?

During a global media conference she attended a session on AI-driven lifelong learning. The speaker described adaptive education platforms enabling mid- and late-life career transitions across industries. Participants shared stories of individuals retraining in entirely new fields beyond fifty or sixty. The idea unsettled Sophia. Reinvention at her age felt improbable. Yet the notion lingered, challenging the assumption that professional identity must remain fixed after midlife.

Months later Sophia enrolled experimentally in an online course on environmental data analysis—an area intersecting journalism and emerging technology. The AI-guided curriculum adapted to her background, linking statistical concepts to narrative frameworks she understood. Progress came faster than she expected. Decades of investigative thinking translated into pattern recognition skills valuable in data interpretation. She discovered satisfaction in mastering unfamiliar tools. Learning revived a sense of expansion she had not felt since early adulthood.

Encouraged, Sophia pursued further modules, integrating data analytics with environmental policy communication. Her prior career, once perceived as obsolete, became foundation rather than barrier. She began consulting on translating complex climate data into public narratives. Organizations sought her hybrid expertise—journalistic storytelling combined with analytical insight. Sophia realized she had not changed careers entirely; she had extended it into a new dimension.

Over the next decade Sophia's work evolved again. She collaborated with AI developers designing communication interfaces for scientific data, ensuring outputs were understandable to policymakers and communities. Her experience across media and advocacy informed system design. Younger colleagues valued her contextual knowledge of public discourse across decades. Age became asset rather than limitation. Sophia inhabited a new professional identity born from the intersection of past and present skills.

Approaching seventy, Sophia embarked on yet another transformation. Witnessing the educational potential of data storytelling, she began teaching short courses on environmental communication through global learning platforms. Students ranged from young activists to mid-career professionals. Sophia guided them in translating data into narratives shaping public action. Teaching brought fulfillment distinct from earlier roles. She saw knowledge multiply through others, extending impact beyond personal output.

Sophia often reflected on how many lives she had lived within one lifespan. Journalist, communications strategist, data analyst, educator—each identity emerged sequentially yet connected. Earlier experiences enriched later ones. The possibility of reinvention had expanded her horizon beyond what she once believed feasible. Longevity had not merely extended time; it had multiplied opportunity for transformation.

At seventy-five Sophia attended a reunion of former colleagues from her journalism years. Many had retired fully, proud of accomplished careers but detached from current professional landscapes. They expressed admiration for her continued engagement. Sophia realized that her trajectory differed not in ambition but in expectation. She had come to view career as evolving continuum rather than finite arc. Health and learning capacity had enabled repeated renewal.

One evening after teaching an international cohort online, Sophia walked along the coast near her home. The horizon stretched wide under fading light. She contemplated the arc of decades ahead—not defined by single profession but by continued curiosity. She might yet explore new domains, integrate emerging technologies, or mentor global networks. Her identity no longer depended on one career label. It rested on adaptability itself.

Sophia understood that the 100-year career was not about working endlessly but about remaining capable of becoming. Each phase of life could host new purpose when health and learning persisted. She felt gratitude for years that allowed multiple beginnings. Her story demonstrated that a long life need not repeat itself; it could diversify.

As waves moved steadily against the shore, Sophia considered the generations behind her. Many had been forced into single career arcs by shorter healthspan and rigid expectations. She lived in a different era—one where longevity and AI opened landscapes of possibility across decades. She turned homeward, preparing for another day of teaching, learning, and becoming. In the century-scale career unfolding before her, she had already lived many lives in one—and sensed there were more yet to come.

Chapter 7

Longevity Wealth: How Extended Lifespans Are Transforming Asset Growth, Compounding, and Financial Power Across Generations

Wealth has always been shaped by time. The fundamental principle of compounding—where returns generate additional returns over successive periods—relies on duration as much as rate. Artificial intelligence–enabled longevity extends the duration component of wealth creation in unprecedented ways. As individuals remain economically active and financially engaged across longer lifespans, asset accumulation and compounding operate over expanded horizons. The concept of longevity wealth emerges: financial power derived not solely from income or investment performance but from sustained participation in economic systems across extended timeframes. In the AI longevity era, wealth increasingly reflects how long capital and capability remain active rather than how intensely they are applied within shorter spans.

Traditional financial planning assumed a predictable lifecycle: accumulation during working years, stabilization near retirement, and gradual decumulation thereafter. Extended healthspan and prolonged earning capacity disrupt this sequence by lengthening the accumulation phase and delaying decumulation. Individuals may continue generating income, investing, and reinvesting well beyond historical retirement ages. The compounding period expands from decades into half-century or longer horizons. Even modest annual returns, when applied across extended durations, produce exponential differences in wealth outcomes. Longevity thus amplifies the temporal engine underlying financial growth.

AI plays a critical role in enabling longevity wealth by optimizing decision-making across extended horizons. Algorithmic portfolio management adapts asset allocation dynamically based on evolving lifespan projections, risk tolerance, and income patterns. Predictive analytics identify optimal investment timing, diversification strategies, and withdrawal schedules aligned with extended productivity. Financial behavior nudging systems encourage consistent contributions and long-term discipline. Over decades, these AI-assisted optimizations compound alongside financial returns, enhancing total wealth accumulation. Longevity wealth therefore arises from both extended duration and improved financial precision.

Extended lifespans also reshape labor income patterns contributing to asset growth. Rather than peaking midlife and declining thereafter, income streams may persist or diversify into later decades through flexible employment, consulting, entrepreneurship, or intellectual property generation. Sustained income allows continued investment contributions beyond traditional retirement thresholds. Asset growth thus benefits not only from time but from prolonged capital inflow. The distinction between accumulation and retirement phases blurs as earning and investing overlap across extended periods. Longevity wealth reflects continuous engagement rather than segmented lifecycle stages.

Intergenerational wealth dynamics transform under extended longevity. Historically, wealth transfer occurred relatively early as older generations passed assets to heirs. Longer lifespans delay inheritance, enabling older individuals to accumulate assets longer and retain financial autonomy. Families may span multiple active economic generations simultaneously, each contributing to and benefiting from shared capital pools. Wealth becomes multi-generational in operation rather than sequential in transfer. AI-assisted estate planning models optimize distribution across extended family timelines, balancing autonomy with legacy. Longevity wealth thus evolves into family-level economic systems spanning decades of overlapping participation. Asset classes themselves adapt to longevity horizons. Investments with long maturation periods—real estate development, infrastructure, private equity, intellectual property portfolios—become more attractive when investors anticipate extended timeframes to realize returns. Longevity capital favors durable, long-duration assets capable of compounding across decades. AI analytics evaluate lifespan-adjusted investment strategies aligning asset duration with investor longevity. Financial markets may increasingly value patience and stability over short-term turnover as investor horizons lengthen. Longevity wealth encourages strategic rather than speculative capital deployment.

Healthcare costs and longevity wealth intersect through preservation of asset usability. Financial wealth has limited value if health decline prevents its application. Extended healthspan ensures that accumulated resources remain usable across longer periods, enhancing real utility of wealth. AI-driven preventive health thus indirectly protects financial capital by preserving functional lifespan. Individuals able to remain active longer can manage investments, pursue opportunities, and adapt strategies across decades. Longevity wealth therefore integrates biological and financial capital: healthspan sustains engagement with accumulated assets.

However, longevity wealth risks amplifying inequality if extended compounding periods concentrate among populations with access to longevity technologies and financial optimization tools. Individuals with longer healthy lifespans accumulate assets longer, reinvest returns, and delay decumulation, widening wealth gaps relative to those with shorter healthspans. Lifespan inequality thus translates directly into wealth inequality. Early access to longevity and financial AI tools magnifies advantage through decades of compounding. Inclusive access to preventive health and financial literacy becomes essential to prevent concentration of longevity wealth among already advantaged groups.

Public policy implications emerge as longevity wealth expands. Tax systems designed around shorter accumulation phases may require adjustment to account for prolonged asset growth. Retirement account structures and contribution limits assume finite earning windows; extended careers may necessitate flexible contribution frameworks. Inheritance taxation models confront delayed transfer patterns. Governments must balance incentives for long-term saving with equitable distribution. AI economic modeling assists policymakers in forecasting longevity-driven wealth trends and designing responsive frameworks. Longevity wealth reshapes fiscal landscapes alongside personal finance.

The psychological dimension of wealth also evolves under extended lifespans. Individuals perceive financial planning across longer horizons, encouraging patience and strategic thinking. Risk tolerance may adjust as recovery time from losses extends across decades. Wealth goals shift from securing retirement to sustaining multi-phase life engagement. Financial identity expands beyond provider-to-retiree transitions into continuous stewardship of capital across lifetime. Longevity wealth becomes narrative of sustained economic agency rather than culmination of accumulation alone.

Ultimately, longevity wealth represents the financial manifestation of extended lifespan. Time multiplies compounding, sustained income prolongs accumulation, and AI optimizes decisions across decades. Wealth becomes increasingly determined by duration of participation rather than intensity of short-term effort. Individuals who understand and harness longevity wealth align health, learning, and financial strategy across extended horizons. Societies that enable broad access to longevity capital distribute compounding opportunity more equitably. In the AI longevity era, financial power grows not merely from what one earns, but from how long one remains able to earn, invest, and compound across life.

The Quiet Compounding

When Daniel Okafor arrived in the country at age twenty-three, he possessed little beyond education, determination, and a willingness to work tirelessly. He took his first job in logistics management, sending a portion of each paycheck home while saving modestly. Wealth seemed distant; survival and stability dominated early years. Yet Daniel carried an internal conviction that time, used consistently, could transform circumstance. He invested small amounts regularly, believing compounding would reward patience even if progress appeared slow.

Decades passed. Daniel advanced professionally, married, raised children, and purchased a modest home. His investments grew gradually, rarely dramatically. He viewed wealth as steady accumulation rather than sudden gain. By his mid-fifties he had achieved financial comfort but not extraordinary assets. Retirement planning began to occupy attention, following traditional expectations of gradual withdrawal from work.

Yet Daniel's health trajectory diverged from those expectations. Consistent exercise, preventive medical care, and balanced living preserved vitality. At sixty-five he remained energetic, cognitively sharp, and professionally respected. Rather than retiring fully, he transitioned into consulting roles within logistics systems design. His expertise, honed over decades, commanded demand. Income continued alongside investment growth. Daniel realized that his compounding period had not ended; it had extended. With continued earnings, Daniel increased investments beyond what retirement would have allowed. Compounding accelerated not through higher risk but through prolonged contribution. His financial timeline expanded by decades he once assumed would be non-earning. The difference, though subtle yearly, became profound cumulatively. Longevity had stretched the quiet process he had trusted since youth.

Family dynamics shifted as well. Daniel's children, now adults, observed his sustained engagement and financial discipline. Rather than awaiting inheritance, they collaborated in family investments, pooling resources into real estate and entrepreneurial ventures. Wealth became shared enterprise across generations rather than deferred transfer. Daniel mentored them in patience and strategy, emphasizing duration over speculation. Longevity allowed guidance to persist while capital grew.

At seventy-two Daniel launched a small logistics optimization firm with former colleagues, leveraging decades of experience and modern AI tools. The venture required minimal capital but generated steady returns. Entrepreneurship, once deemed late, felt natural within extended healthspan. Profits reinvested alongside existing assets, compounding anew. Daniel marveled that his most financially productive years occurred beyond traditional retirement age. Walking through his neighborhood years later, Daniel reflected on how quietly his wealth had grown. No dramatic windfalls, only sustained engagement and time extended by health. He realized that longevity itself had been multiplier. Without continued vitality he would have ceased earning and investing decades earlier. Instead, the compounding he trusted had simply continued. Longevity wealth had emerged not from extraordinary strategy but from extended participation.

At eighty Daniel remained active, advising family ventures and managing investments with clarity. His assets supported grandchildren's education and community projects he valued. Wealth now expressed itself through impact as much as security. He recognized that his financial journey illustrated a broader truth: when healthy years extend, compounding deepens. Time, faithfully applied, becomes the quiet architect of prosperity.

One evening Daniel reviewed early account statements from his twenties. The amounts were small, almost symbolic compared with present figures. Yet those early contributions, sustained and extended across decades of unexpected productivity, had multiplied beyond youthful imagination. Longevity had not changed his discipline; it had prolonged it. The quiet compounding continued.

As he closed the records, Daniel felt gratitude for years that allowed patience to mature into abundance. His life demonstrated that wealth often grows not in bursts but in continuance. Extended lifespan had allowed continuance beyond expectation. In that extension lay the true power of longevity wealth—the capacity of time itself to accumulate value when health and engagement endure.

Chapter 8

The Longevity Economy: How Longer Healthy Lives Are Reshaping Markets, Industries, and Global Economic Growth

The extension of human healthspan does not merely alter individual life trajectories; it reorganizes entire economic systems. When populations live longer in good health, consumption patterns, labor participation, innovation cycles, and industrial demand structures shift simultaneously. This systemic transformation is often termed the longevity economy: the aggregate economic activity generated by individuals whose extended lifespans sustain engagement across decades once associated with decline. Artificial intelligence accelerates and amplifies this phenomenon by preserving capability, enabling productivity, and facilitating participation across longer life stages. As societies transition from aging populations to long-lived populations, markets evolve from serving late-life dependency toward supporting prolonged vitality, learning, and contribution.

Traditional economic models segmented life stages into production and consumption phases. Younger and middle-aged adults produced income and accumulated assets, while older adults consumed savings and healthcare services with limited productivity. Extended healthspan dissolves this dichotomy. Older individuals remain active earners, consumers, entrepreneurs, and innovators simultaneously. Economic participation becomes continuous across lifespan rather than concentrated in midlife. This continuity expands aggregate demand and supply concurrently. Populations previously considered economically inactive remain contributors, enlarging markets without demographic expansion. Longevity thus acts as endogenous growth driver.

Healthcare and wellness industries sit at the core of the longevity economy. Preventive health technologies, AI diagnostics, personalized nutrition, regenerative medicine, and cognitive enhancement services expand rapidly as individuals invest in maintaining capability across longer lives. Demand shifts from acute treatment toward continuous optimization. Health becomes proactive lifestyle infrastructure rather than episodic intervention. Markets emerge around monitoring devices, data analytics platforms, and longevity therapeutics. Economic value migrates from late-stage care institutions to preventive ecosystems. The healthcare sector transforms from managing decline to sustaining performance. Education and skill development industries also expand dramatically under extended lifespans. Lifelong learning becomes necessity rather than optional enrichment as individuals pursue multiple career phases across decades. AI-driven adaptive education platforms deliver continuous training accessible at any age. Universities and training providers evolve into lifelong service institutions offering modular credentials and recurrent programs. Midlife and late-life education markets grow alongside youth education. Knowledge economies benefit from sustained human capital renewal across extended timelines. The longevity economy thus integrates education as permanent component of economic participation.

Housing and urban development sectors respond to extended vitality by designing environments supporting multi-decade occupancy and active aging. Demand rises for adaptable homes accommodating evolving needs without institutionalization. Mixed-age communities integrate recreation, healthcare access, and learning infrastructure. Longevity-oriented urban planning prioritizes walkability, accessibility, and wellness integration. Real estate markets shift from retirement-centric communities toward lifespan-inclusive living environments. AI analytics guide planning based on demographic healthspan projections, optimizing infrastructure investment. Housing becomes longevity-supportive asset rather than static shelter.

Consumer markets diversify as extended healthy years sustain spending power across older demographics. Travel, leisure, technology, education, and lifestyle industries experience growth driven by active older consumers. Consumption patterns resemble those of midlife populations rather than dependency-driven spending. Businesses increasingly design products and services for longevity demographics: experiential travel, cognitive fitness platforms, lifelong hobbies, and wellness technologies. Marketing narratives shift from anti-aging to pro-longevity messaging emphasizing capability and engagement. The longevity consumer becomes central economic actor.

Labor markets expand participation across broader age ranges, increasing economic output and tax bases. Extended workforce engagement described in earlier chapters translates into sustained production capacity at macro scale. Economies facing declining birth rates offset demographic contraction through prolonged worker participation. Experience-rich labor enhances productivity in knowledge-intensive sectors. AI tools facilitate flexible employment and collaboration across age groups, integrating longevity into workforce design. The longevity economy thus stabilizes growth in aging societies by converting additional healthy years into productive contribution.

Innovation ecosystems benefit uniquely from longevity dynamics. Extended careers allow individuals to accumulate deep expertise before pursuing entrepreneurship or research breakthroughs. Mature innovators combine decades of experience with contemporary technology, generating solutions grounded in long-term perspective. AI collaboration platforms connect multi-generational teams, integrating youthful creativity with seasoned insight. Extended lifespan increases probability of high-impact innovation events across lifetime. Societies harnessing longevity capital thus gain competitive advantage in research and technological advancement.

Financial services industries adapt to longevity-driven economic structures. Investment products align with extended horizons, emphasizing long-duration assets and adaptive income streams. Insurance models incorporate healthspan metrics and preventive incentives. Retirement planning evolves into lifelong financial management integrating earning, investing, and phased independence. Longevity risk assessment becomes core financial discipline. AI financial analytics personalize strategies across extended lifespans. Financial markets increasingly recognize longevity as macroeconomic variable influencing asset demand and capital flows.

Global economic patterns also shift as longevity gains vary across regions. Nations investing early in AI-driven preventive health and education infrastructure capture longevity dividends and extended workforce participation. These societies experience sustained productivity and consumer demand despite aging demographics. Regions lacking longevity infrastructure face continued health burdens and reduced participation. Global competitiveness increasingly correlates with population healthspan rather than population size alone. Longevity economics becomes dimension of geopolitical strategy alongside technology and education.

However, the longevity economy introduces structural transition challenges. Industries built around late-life dependency may contract as preventive health reduces disease burden. Pension systems and healthcare financing must adapt to prolonged participation. Workforce integration across age groups requires cultural and institutional change. Markets must avoid reinforcing lifespan inequality by ensuring longevity products remain accessible. Policymakers must balance innovation incentives with equity goals. The transition from aging economy to longevity economy involves reallocation of resources across sectors rather than uniform growth.

Ultimately, the longevity economy represents systemic reorganization of markets around extended human capability. AI enables preservation of healthspan and productivity, converting additional years into sustained economic participation. Consumption, production, innovation, and investment patterns adjust to longer lives lived actively. Societies that align infrastructure, policy, and markets with longevity realities unlock new growth potential. The longevity economy is not merely an extension of existing systems but an evolution toward economic structures centered on sustained human vitality. In the AI longevity era, growth arises not only from technological progress but from the expansion of capable years across populations.

The City of Long Lives

When urban planner Lucia Ferreira first arrived in Porto Claro as a young architect, the city reflected familiar demographic patterns. Youth dominated public spaces, while older residents occupied quieter neighborhoods and healthcare facilities. Infrastructure assumed gradual withdrawal from active life after mid-sixties. Retirement complexes lined suburban edges, separated from commercial and educational centers. The city functioned efficiently within assumptions of shorter healthspan. Lucia designed projects accordingly, unaware how profoundly those assumptions would change.

Decades later, as longevity initiatives spread nationally, Porto Claro began to transform. Preventive health programs, AI monitoring systems, and accessible lifelong education extended vitality across older populations. Citizens remained active into seventies and eighties. Traditional retirement enclaves emptied as residents returned to central districts seeking engagement. The demographic map shifted from segmented age zones toward integrated participation. Lucia, now a senior planner, confronted a city evolving beyond earlier design logic.

Her team initiated studies on longevity-driven urban needs. Data revealed rising participation of older adults in work, education, and recreation. Public transit usage extended across age groups, while demand for adaptive housing increased. Healthcare visits shifted toward preventive services integrated into community spaces. Lucia realized that Porto Claro was transitioning from aging city to longevity city—one designed for sustained capability rather than managed decline.

She led development of mixed-age districts combining residential, educational, health, and commercial functions. Buildings incorporated adaptable interiors allowing residents to age in place without relocation. Public spaces emphasized walkability, exercise, and social interaction across generations. Lifelong learning centers replaced traditional retirement clubs.

Technology infrastructure enabled remote work and telehealth seamlessly across homes. The city began reflecting continuous participation rather than life-stage segregation.

As projects unfolded, Lucia observed unexpected cultural change. Older residents launched businesses, attended university courses, and mentored youth programs. Markets thrived on diverse consumer groups active simultaneously. Cafés filled with intergenerational collaboration. The economy expanded not from population growth but from prolonged engagement. Porto Claro's GDP rose steadily despite stable demographics. Lucia recognized the longevity economy embodied in urban form.

Personally, Lucia experienced the shift as well. Approaching seventy, she remained professionally active, advising international cities on longevity planning. Her own healthspan, supported by preventive programs, sustained energy and creativity. She realized that extended capability had enabled her to guide transformation she might once have retired before witnessing. Longevity extended not only years but influence across her field.

Walking through a newly completed district one afternoon, Lucia watched scenes unimaginable in her youth: older adults exercising beside children, midlife professionals attending evening classes, elders managing local startups. The city pulsed with sustained vitality across age. She understood that infrastructure had both responded to and reinforced longevity economics. Urban design shaped participation just as participation shaped markets. Years later Porto Claro gained global recognition as model longevity city. Delegations visited to study integrated health, education, housing, and workforce systems. Lucia presented planning principles rooted in extended healthspan reality. Cities worldwide began adapting similar frameworks. The longevity economy moved from theory to lived environment. Lucia felt quiet pride knowing her work had helped reimagine how cities function across longer lives.

On her eightieth birthday Lucia walked the riverfront promenade she had redesigned decades earlier. Cafés, learning hubs, and wellness centers lined the path, filled with people of all ages engaged in commerce and culture. The atmosphere conveyed continuity rather than generational succession. She realized the city itself embodied the story of long lives—economy, infrastructure, and culture aligned with extended human capability.

As evening light reflected on the water, Lucia considered the arc of her own life within the city's transformation. She had begun designing for populations expected to decline; she ended shaping environments sustaining vitality. Longevity had rewritten both urban economics and personal horizons. Porto Claro stood as living testament that when healthy years expand, cities and economies expand with them. The city of long lives was not future speculation—it was present reality unfolding across extended human time.

Chapter 9

The Multi-Generational Economy: How Longer Lives Are Reshaping Families, Wealth Transfer, and Economic Collaboration Across Generations

Human societies have always been organized around generational succession. Economic roles, wealth transfer, and social authority traditionally shifted from older to younger cohorts as aging reduced capability and mortality created turnover. Artificial intelligence–enabled longevity alters this temporal rhythm fundamentally by extending healthspan and sustaining capability across overlapping generations. Families and societies increasingly contain four, five, or even six economically active age cohorts simultaneously. This demographic layering produces a multi-generational economy in which production, consumption, innovation, and wealth creation occur concurrently across extended age ranges rather than sequentially through generational replacement.

The traditional generational model assumed predictable transitions: older adults retired, transferred assets, and ceded roles to younger participants. Extended healthspan disrupts this cycle by delaying both retirement and inheritance. Older generations remain economically active, retaining income streams, decision authority, and capital stewardship longer. Younger generations enter adulthood within family systems where elders remain contributors rather than dependents. Economic roles become collaborative rather than sequential. Families function as multi-age economic units with overlapping participation in labor, investment, and enterprise across decades. Longevity transforms generational turnover into generational integration.

Wealth dynamics shift profoundly under this structure. Inheritance historically redistributed capital from older to younger cohorts relatively early in adult life. Longer lifespans postpone transfer, allowing assets to compound under older ownership while younger generations build independent wealth streams. Families may operate shared investment strategies across generations, pooling resources into long-term assets such as real estate portfolios, businesses, or intellectual property. AI-assisted financial planning models multi-generational timelines, optimizing contributions, distributions, and stewardship roles across extended family horizons. Wealth becomes distributed across time rather than passed once at death. The economic unit of analysis expands from individual lifecycle to family lifespan. Labor collaboration across generations also intensifies. Extended workforce participation keeps experienced individuals active alongside younger workers for decades longer than before. Intergenerational teams integrate accumulated expertise with emerging knowledge. AI collaboration platforms facilitate knowledge exchange independent of age or geography, enabling mentorship and co-creation across cohorts. Organizations increasingly value age diversity as productivity enhancer rather than liability. Multi-generational labor pools stabilize institutional knowledge and innovation continuity. Economic productivity becomes cumulative across generations rather than replaced periodically.

Entrepreneurship within families evolves accordingly. Longer healthy lives allow older members to launch ventures later while younger members contribute technical skills and market awareness. Family enterprises span age cohorts with complementary capabilities: strategic experience, operational execution, and digital fluency. Longevity reduces urgency of succession planning, allowing gradual transition of leadership and ownership. Businesses persist across generations without abrupt discontinuity. Multi-generational entrepreneurship leverages extended timelines for venture maturation and resilience. AI tools support coordination, governance, and financial transparency across distributed family stakeholders.

Education patterns adapt to multi-generational participation. Lifelong learning across age cohorts creates households where multiple generations engage in education simultaneously. Knowledge flows bidirectionally: elders share experience while younger members share technological literacy. AI learning platforms personalize curricula for each age group within shared environments. Families become learning ecosystems rather than hierarchical instruction chains. This dynamic enhances human capital accumulation across generations and sustains adaptability across extended timelines. Education becomes collective endeavor rather than age-bounded stage.

Caregiving structures also transform. Traditionally, caregiving flowed downward from midlife adults to aging parents and upward to children. Extended healthspan reduces late-life dependency and distributes caregiving responsibilities across longer spans. Older adults remain caregivers for grandchildren or community members while younger adults support midlife transitions. Multi-generational households or networks share responsibilities flexibly. AI-enabled health monitoring and remote care tools support independence, reducing burden concentration. Economic productivity benefits when fewer adults withdraw from labor to provide intensive care prematurely. Longevity thus redistributes caregiving across time.

Societal institutions must adapt to sustained multi-generational participation. Political representation, corporate governance, and cultural leadership historically cycled across generations as elders exited roles. Extended participation may slow turnover, potentially constraining advancement opportunities for younger cohorts. Balancing continuity with renewal requires structural innovation: term limits, advisory roles, and mentorship pathways allowing experienced individuals to contribute without monopolizing authority. AI analytics can model leadership diversity across age groups, guiding equitable participation. The multi-generational economy thrives when integration complements mobility rather than obstructing it.

Housing and urban design respond to multi-generational living patterns. Demand rises for adaptable homes accommodating extended family presence without overcrowding. Co-living models integrate private and shared spaces across age groups. Community infrastructure supports intergenerational interaction through shared learning, recreation, and care facilities. Cities become networks of age-integrated neighborhoods rather than segregated retirement zones. Longevity reshapes spatial economics of living arrangements as families maintain proximity across extended timelines. Housing markets evolve toward flexibility and inclusivity.

Inequality considerations emerge prominently within multi-generational economies. Families with extended healthspan and longevity wealth accumulate advantages across generations simultaneously, reinforcing socioeconomic status. Others experiencing shorter healthspans may lose intergenerational support and mentorship earlier. Policy frameworks addressing education access, preventive healthcare, and wealth distribution influence whether multi-generational longevity reduces or exacerbates inequality. Inclusive longevity systems enable all families to sustain participation across generations. Without equity, longevity advantages concentrate within already privileged lineages.

Culturally, the multi-generational economy alters perceptions of age and authority. Experience retains value across longer spans, but innovation flows continuously from younger cohorts. Social narratives shift from generational replacement to generational collaboration. Identity becomes less age-bounded as individuals witness capability across extended decades. Families experience continuity rather than succession. Economic relationships reflect partnership rather than dependency across age groups. Longevity thus reshapes social cohesion alongside economic structure.

Ultimately, the multi-generational economy represents demographic and economic convergence of extended lifespans.

Families and societies operate across overlapping cohorts of sustained capability, integrating production, consumption, and wealth creation across decades simultaneously. AI enables coordination of financial, educational, and collaborative systems across extended timelines. Societies that embrace generational integration harness accumulated human capital and shared longevity wealth. In the AI longevity era, economic life is no longer handed from one generation to the next—it is built together across many at once.

All the Years Together

The Rao family home had always been full, but in recent years fullness took on new meaning. Three generations had once lived there sequentially—grandparents aging, parents raising children, then children leaving to build lives elsewhere. Yet as longevity extended health and vitality across age, the pattern shifted. At seventy-six, Arun Rao still managed the family textile business with strategic clarity. His daughter Meera, forty-eight, oversaw operations. Meera's son Kiran, twenty-three, recently returned from university with expertise in digital commerce. Instead of succession, collaboration unfolded.

Arun remembered his own father relinquishing control in his sixties due to declining health. Leadership had passed abruptly to the next generation. Arun had expected similar transition.

Yet his sustained vitality allowed continued engagement. He provided long-range strategy and supplier relationships built over decades. Meera directed production and workforce management. Kiran introduced AI-driven logistics and global online marketing. Three generations operated simultaneously, each contributing distinct capability. The business expanded faster than any single generation could have achieved alone.

Family meetings reflected this integration. Decisions blended Arun's experience, Meera's operational insight, and Kiran's technological innovation. Authority became shared rather than transferred. Profit distribution supported both reinvestment and individual goals across generations. Longevity extended Arun's participation while enabling mentorship and continuity. The enterprise embodied multi-generational economy in practice.

Beyond business, family life also changed. Arun remained physically active, traveling with grandchildren and teaching them traditional craft techniques. Meera pursued executive education midlife, inspired by her father's sustained learning. Kiran lived temporarily at home while launching new ventures. The household contained simultaneous growth phases rather than sequential stages. Years overlapped rather than replaced each other.

As prosperity grew, the family invested jointly in community projects—schools, health clinics, artisan cooperatives. Longevity allowed elders to guide philanthropic vision while younger members executed implementation. Impact multiplied across age cohorts. Arun saw in these projects a continuation of legacy not postponed until inheritance but enacted collectively during life. Wealth and purpose flowed across generations concurrently.

At eighty-two Arun began gradually reducing operational involvement, transitioning into advisory role while Meera assumed full leadership. The shift occurred organically, not forced by incapacity. Kiran expanded digital markets internationally. The business now spanned three active generations and prepared to include a fourth as Kiran's daughter grew. Succession had become continuum rather than rupture.

One evening the family gathered on the veranda overlooking fields supplying their textiles. Arun watched Meera and Kiran discussing expansion plans animatedly. He felt no urgency to withdraw, only satisfaction witnessing continuity. Longevity had allowed him to remain present through transformations once unseen by predecessors. His father had not lived to see grandchildren enter business; Arun did. Years together enriched both family and enterprise.

Meera reflected privately on the unusual privilege of working alongside her father for decades rather than inheriting suddenly. His mentorship shaped her leadership deeply. She anticipated guiding Kiran similarly across extended years. Longevity replaced generational gaps with bridges. Knowledge transmission occurred through shared experience rather than memory alone.

Kiran, representing youngest cohort, viewed multi-generational collaboration as natural. He had grown within network of elders active and engaged, not distant retirees. Their presence normalized lifelong contribution. He felt neither pressure to replace nor impatience to advance prematurely. Instead he valued partnership across age. Longevity culture shaped his expectations of work and family.

As dusk settled, Arun spoke softly to family gathered around. "Our years did not pass separately," he said. "They joined." The phrase captured essence of multi-generational economy lived intimately. Extended healthspan had allowed lives to overlap richly rather than sequentially. Wealth, knowledge, and purpose flowed across generations simultaneously.

Years later, after Arun's peaceful passing at ninety-one, the family business continued seamlessly. Meera and Kiran guided it forward, carrying decades of shared experience. They felt not loss of abrupt succession but completion of long collaboration. Arun's presence remained embedded in systems and values cultivated together. Longevity had allowed legacy to mature across time shared rather than time divided.

Standing in the workshop one morning, Kiran watched artisans weaving fabric patterns his great-grandfather once designed. He realized the enterprise embodied all the years together—four generations intertwined through sustained vitality. The multi-generational economy was not abstract theory but lived continuity of family, work, and time extended across lives.

Chapter 10

The Longevity Future of Wealth and Work: How AI-Extended Lifespans Are Redefining Human Value, Economic Systems, and the Meaning of Prosperity

As artificial intelligence extends human healthspan and capability across unprecedented durations, the relationship between time, work, and wealth enters a structural transformation that extends beyond incremental economic change. Earlier chapters have explored how extended lifespan reshapes careers, retirement, markets, families, and capital accumulation. The convergence of these forces reveals a broader redefinition: prosperity in the longevity era is no longer determined primarily by peak productivity within a short working life but by sustained capability across extended years. The longevity future of wealth and work emerges from this shift, where human value is measured less by intensity of output and more by duration of meaningful contribution.

Historically, economic systems optimized around scarcity of productive time. Education compressed learning into youth, careers concentrated output into midlife, and retirement signaled withdrawal from economic participation. Artificial intelligence–enabled longevity dissolves this scarcity by extending functional years and enabling continuous adaptation. Time itself expands as usable economic resource. Individuals remain capable of learning, producing, investing, and innovating across decades previously lost to decline. Wealth creation therefore becomes temporal rather than episodic. Sustained participation replaces concentrated effort as the primary driver of prosperity.

The longevity future integrates biological capital with financial and intellectual capital. Healthspan preservation ensures that accumulated knowledge and wealth remain actionable across longer horizons. AI health optimization delays functional decline, while AI learning systems sustain cognitive growth. Together they preserve agency across lifespan. Human capital no longer depreciates predictably with age; instead, it may appreciate through compounded experience. Economic systems adapt by valuing continuity of capability rather than youth-centric productivity. Longevity thus stabilizes and amplifies human value across time.

Work itself undergoes conceptual transformation. Instead of finite careers bounded by retirement, individuals engage in iterative cycles of creation, education, entrepreneurship, mentorship, and reinvention across extended timelines. The boundary between working and nonworking life dissolves into variable engagement intensity. AI tools facilitate flexible participation independent of location, physical strength, or fixed schedules. Work becomes less about survival and more about expression of expertise and purpose across lifespan. The longevity future reframes labor from necessity to elective contribution enabled by sustained capability.

Wealth creation similarly shifts from accumulation followed by decumulation to continuous stewardship across extended life. Individuals generate income, invest, and reinvest across decades beyond traditional retirement. Financial independence becomes capacity to choose engagement rather than cease work entirely. AI financial planning integrates healthspan projections and multi-phase careers into dynamic asset strategies. Longevity wealth accumulates not merely through returns but through prolonged contribution and compounding. Prosperity reflects sustained participation rather than early-life advantage alone.

Economic institutions must adapt comprehensively to this redefinition. Pension systems transition from age-based entitlements to capability-sensitive frameworks. Education systems become lifelong service platforms supporting repeated skill acquisition. Healthcare shifts from episodic treatment to continuous optimization preserving productivity. Labor markets incorporate flexible roles accommodating extended participation. Financial systems recognize longevity as central variable shaping asset demand and capital flows. The longevity future requires integrated institutional redesign aligning with extended human timelines.

At the societal level, extended lifespan alters distribution of opportunity and responsibility. Individuals possess longer horizons for personal development and contribution, but also extended responsibility for sustaining health, learning, and economic engagement. Societies must provide accessible preventive health, lifelong education, and adaptable work structures to ensure longevity translates into shared prosperity rather than stratified advantage. Equity in longevity capital determines whether extended lifespan benefits all or concentrates among privileged populations. The longevity future of wealth depends on inclusive access to extended capability.

Cultural narratives of aging transform alongside economic structures. Aging ceases to signify decline and withdrawal; it represents accumulation and extended possibility. Societies recognizing this shift unlock human capital across decades previously marginalized. Individuals redefine identity across life stages, pursuing new ambitions beyond traditional midlife peaks. Psychological horizons expand as people anticipate extended capacity for growth. The longevity future thus reshapes not only economic systems but human self-perception.

Artificial intelligence functions as both catalyst and coordinator in this transformation. AI health systems preserve functional lifespan; AI learning systems sustain adaptability; AI labor platforms enable flexible participation; AI financial analytics optimize extended wealth creation. These interconnected systems convert biological longevity into economic longevity. Without AI integration, extended lifespan alone might increase dependency. With AI, extended lifespan amplifies capability and productivity. The longevity future of wealth and work arises from this synergy between biological extension and technological augmentation.

Global economic implications extend beyond individual prosperity. Nations with longevity-enhanced populations gain sustained workforce participation, reduced healthcare burden, and extended innovation cycles. Economic growth derives not solely from population expansion but from expanded productive lifespan per individual. Demographic aging no longer implies economic contraction when healthspan extends. Longevity economies become engines of stability in aging societies. Global competitiveness increasingly correlates with population healthspan and lifelong education infrastructure. The longevity future of wealth thus operates at macroeconomic scale.

Ethical considerations accompany this transformation. If extended capability becomes determinant of prosperity, unequal access to longevity technologies risks entrenching inequality across generations. Societies must ensure that extended lifespan does not produce biological class divisions where some populations live longer, learn longer, and accumulate more. Inclusive longevity policy becomes economic necessity. The future of wealth in the longevity era depends on equitable distribution of healthspan and learning opportunity. Prosperity must be measured not only by aggregate wealth but by shared years of capability.

Ultimately, the longevity future of wealth and work converges on a central insight: time, when preserved and extended, becomes the most powerful multiplier of human value. Individuals able to sustain health, learning, and engagement across decades accumulate not only financial capital but experiential, intellectual, and social capital that compounds across life. Economic systems that recognize and support this sustained capability unlock unprecedented human potential. Prosperity in the AI longevity era emerges from the integration of extended life with extended contribution. Wealth becomes not endpoint of a career but expression of a life lived fully across time.

A Life That Keeps Opening

Elias Navarro had once believed that life unfolded in three clear acts: preparation, achievement, and rest. Raised in a family where elders slowed visibly after sixty, he assumed his own arc would mirror theirs. He built a career in manufacturing engineering, rising steadily through technical and managerial roles. By his early sixties he felt accomplished and prepared for retirement. Financial plans were secure, children independent, and work demands exhausting. He anticipated the quiet closure that generations before him had accepted as natural.

Yet retirement did not arrive as he expected. Months after leaving his executive position, Elias found himself restless. His health remained strong, his mind active, and curiosity unquenched. He began exploring emerging technologies he had observed only peripherally during his career—automation analytics, AI manufacturing systems, sustainable production design. Initially he engaged out of interest rather than ambition. But the learning reignited dormant enthusiasm. He realized that knowledge accumulated over decades could interface with new technologies in ways younger specialists lacked.

Encouraged by former colleagues, Elias began advising small manufacturing startups integrating AI optimization into traditional production lines. His experience diagnosing inefficiencies proved invaluable when combined with algorithmic analysis tools. Startups sought his guidance repeatedly. What began as casual consulting evolved into sustained engagement. Elias discovered that his later years offered opportunities distinct from earlier career stages: he could choose projects aligned with curiosity, free from corporate constraints.

As his seventies approached, Elias co-founded a niche consultancy specializing in modernizing mid-sized factories for sustainability and automation. Younger partners handled technical implementation while Elias shaped strategic direction. The venture grew steadily, its success rooted in blending experience with innovation. Elias recognized that his most impactful professional phase had emerged after the age he once considered endpoint. Longevity had extended not merely time but relevance.

Parallel transformations occurred in his personal life. With extended vitality he pursued interests long deferred—learning advanced design software, studying environmental systems, mentoring engineering students. He traveled globally to observe emerging manufacturing ecosystems, connecting with innovators across generations. His sense of identity shifted from retired executive to lifelong engineer engaged in evolving challenges. Retirement, once imagined as closure, became transition into autonomy. At eighty Elias remained intellectually vibrant and physically active. His consultancy transitioned gradually to younger leadership, but he continued advisory roles and educational outreach. Universities invited him to teach short courses on industrial transformation across decades. Students valued his perspective spanning technological eras. Elias felt his life had expanded into phases he once thought impossible. Each decade opened new paths rather than narrowing options.

Reflecting on his journey, Elias realized that prosperity in his later years extended beyond financial security. Wealth now included accumulated insight, relationships, and capacity to contribute meaningfully. Extended lifespan had allowed these forms of capital to mature fully. He saw his life not as three acts but as ongoing unfolding—a sequence of beginnings sustained by health and curiosity.

One evening near his eighty-fifth birthday, Elias stood in his workshop reviewing prototype designs for a sustainable manufacturing process he had helped conceptualize with younger engineers. The project combined decades of mechanical understanding with modern AI optimization. Watching the team collaborate across age and expertise, Elias felt continuity of purpose that transcended generational boundaries. His presence represented not past authority but living contribution. He recalled his father at similar age, withdrawn from work by necessity rather than choice. The difference lay not in character but in era. Elias lived in a time when longevity and technology preserved capability. He felt gratitude for years that kept opening rather than closing. Life had not narrowed into rest; it had diversified into continued creation.

As night settled, Elias wrote in his journal: "I thought life would finish its work and then end. Instead it keeps beginning." The phrase captured his experience of the longevity future. Extended years had allowed reinvention, contribution, and growth beyond expected limits. Prosperity had emerged from sustained engagement rather than early achievement alone.

Looking ahead, Elias felt no urgency to measure remaining time. Whether years were few or many mattered less than knowing each could still hold purpose. His life illustrated the ultimate insight of longevity economics lived personally: when health and learning endure, value continues to grow. A life extended becomes a life that keeps opening.

Epilogue

The Economics of Time

The central economic reality of the longevity era is deceptively simple: when human lives extend in health and capability, time itself becomes the most valuable form of capital. Across this book we have examined how artificial intelligence–enabled longevity reshapes work, wealth, retirement, inequality, families, markets, and institutions. Each domain reflects a common transformation—the expansion of usable years. What emerges is not merely a longer life, but a longer economic life: extended participation in learning, creating, investing, and contributing across decades once lost to decline. The future of prosperity, therefore, depends less on how much individuals can produce within a short span and more on how long they remain capable of producing meaningfully.

For centuries, economies operated under implicit biological constraints. Human productivity rose, peaked, and faded within predictable limits. Wealth accumulation compressed into midlife. Retirement marked withdrawal. Generational turnover ensured continuity. Longevity economics dissolves these patterns by extending the productive horizon outward. Instead of a single career arc followed by cessation, individuals experience multiple cycles of contribution. Instead of a brief accumulation window, wealth compounds across extended decades. Instead of generational succession, families and institutions operate through overlapping participation. Time shifts from constraint to multiplier. The economics of time becomes the defining framework of the longevity age.

Artificial intelligence accelerates this shift by converting added years into usable years. Longevity alone does not guarantee productivity; extended healthspan and adaptability do. AI health systems preserve physiological and cognitive function. AI learning systems sustain skill renewal. AI labor platforms enable flexible engagement. AI financial systems optimize long-horizon wealth creation. Together these technologies transform lifespan extension into economic extension. The longevity era is therefore not simply biological progress but technological integration of health, knowledge, and work across time. Prosperity emerges from sustained capability rather than episodic peak.

This transformation redefines human value itself. In shorter-lived economies, value correlated with early productivity and rapid achievement. In longevity economies, value correlates with continuity of contribution and accumulated insight. Experience compounds alongside capital. Individuals become more valuable over time when health and learning persist. Societies that recognize this shift unlock human capital previously discarded prematurely. Aging populations transform from fiscal burdens into reservoirs of expertise. Longevity reframes aging from decline narrative to accumulation narrative. The meaning of age evolves from limitation to depth.

Economic institutions must adapt accordingly. Retirement systems transition from age-based withdrawal to capability-based flexibility. Education becomes lifelong infrastructure rather than youth phase. Healthcare becomes preventive optimization preserving productivity. Labor markets integrate multi-age participation. Financial systems incorporate extended horizons. Urban environments support prolonged vitality. These adaptations collectively align economies with extended human timelines. The longevity economy thus represents systemic redesign around the expanded human lifespan.

Yet the economics of time carries ethical responsibility. If extended lifespan becomes determinant of prosperity, unequal access to longevity technologies risks creating divisions measured in years of capability. Lifespan inequality could translate into wealth inequality, opportunity inequality, and generational inequality. The future of longevity economics therefore depends on inclusivity. Preventive healthcare, lifelong education, and adaptive employment must scale broadly to ensure extended years benefit entire populations. Shared longevity yields shared prosperity. Unequal longevity yields stratified societies. The distribution of time becomes central justice question of the century.

Across cultures and eras, wealth has often been perceived as accumulation of resources. The longevity era reveals a deeper truth: wealth ultimately derives from sustained time applied with capability. Financial assets, knowledge, relationships, and influence all compound when individuals remain healthy and engaged longer. The expansion of human lifespan therefore expands the potential for all forms of wealth. Prosperity becomes not merely what one earns but how long one remains able to earn, learn, and contribute. Time becomes economic substrate from which all other capital emerges.

For individuals, this realization invites a new orientation toward life planning. Health optimization becomes foundational economic strategy. Lifelong learning becomes investment rather than optional enrichment. Flexible career design replaces single-path progression. Financial planning aligns with extended earning and compounding horizons. Relationships and mentorship gain importance as multi-generational collaboration deepens. The longevity mindset views life as unfolding continuum rather than finite sequence. Economic agency extends across decades of possibility. For societies, the implications are equally profound. Nations that invest in population healthspan, lifelong education, and adaptive institutions harness longevity dividends in productivity, innovation, and stability. Aging demographics cease to threaten growth when healthy lifespan expands. Economies evolve from youth-centric models to lifespan-inclusive systems. Public policy shifts from managing decline to enabling sustained participation. Longevity economics thus offers pathway to prosperity in aging societies worldwide.

The deeper philosophical transformation accompanying these changes concerns humanity's relationship with time itself. For most of history, time was perceived as diminishing resource. Life moved irreversibly toward decline. The longevity era introduces an alternative perception: time as expandable field of possibility when health and capability endure. This does not eliminate mortality or aging, but it extends the period during which individuals can shape outcomes. Economic life becomes less bounded by age and more by intention. The human story gains length and continuity.

Throughout this book we have seen how extended healthspan reshapes careers, retirement, wealth accumulation, markets, families, and global economies. These domains converge on a single insight: the extension of healthy years is among the most powerful economic forces ever encountered. Industrialization multiplied physical productivity. Digitalization multiplied information productivity. Longevity multiplies temporal productivity—the duration over which humans can apply capability. This multiplication transforms the scale of potential contribution across lives and societies.

The future of AI longevity economics ultimately rests on alignment between biological extension and institutional adaptation. If societies redesign systems to support extended capability, the additional years gained through science become years of prosperity, creativity, and shared growth. If institutions lag, extended lifespan risks producing instability and inequality. The challenge of the century is therefore not only extending life but extending meaningful participation within life. Economic structures must evolve as rapidly as longevity technologies.

As we close this exploration, one truth stands clear: the defining resource of the longevity era is not money, technology, or even knowledge—it is time lived capable. The extension of healthy lifespan expands the human horizon. Within that horizon lie decades of learning, creating, mentoring, and building yet to be realized. The economics of time reveals that prosperity grows from sustained engagement across life. When years expand, possibility expands with them. The future economy will be built not only by what humans do, but by how long they remain able to do it.

www.ingramcontent.com/pod-product-compliance
Lightning Source LLC
LaVergne TN
LVHW022228200926
848481LV00006B/2165